DOGS DESERVE DIALOGUE

Rover Should Hang On Your Words
Not On Your Leash

by **Judy Moore**

Illustrated by
Jim Moore

Tyke Publishing

Note to Reader

The purpose of this book is to present ideas and methods which the author has found to be the key to helping all dogs live securely and successfully in a human society. It is the author's hope that this book will guide dog owners into developing a meaningful, happy, functional, and permanent relationship with their dogs. As different dogs have different temperaments, results from employing the methods in this book may vary. These techniques are meant to be used humanely and carefully, and the author does not condone nor take responsibility for any application or misapplication of these techniques which may harm a dog. The author expressly disclaims any and all liability for any injuries and/or other losses resulting from adopting any concepts or ideas presented in this book or from applying the dog training techniques described herein.

If you do not wish to be bound by the above, you may return this book to the publisher for a full refund.

Tyke Publishing, P.O. Box 4132, Buena Vista, CO 81211

ISBN 0-9672868-0-8

About the Author

Judy Moore has been a student of animal behavior all her life. She grew up in a lakeside home in Michigan, rescuing and training everything from ducks to dogs and horses. Judy holds an undergraduate degree in zoology and a masters degree in technical communications, so communicating with animals has always been very natural for her.

While traveling in countries throughout the world, Judy observed firsthand the neglect and abuse of dogs in many human cultures. After a brief career as an editor and writer, she settled with her husband and sons in the Colorado mountains where she owns and operates Wapiti Run, a horse training and breeding ranch, a sanctuary for rescued animals, especially dogs, and the headquarters for her dog owner training program.

Judy was one of the founders and served as director of the Pet Assistance League, a private human organization committed to rescuing, rehabilitating and adopting out abandoned dogs. The PAL also vigorously promoted dog-owner education and responsibility, including dog obedience training.

Her skills in communications research have served her well in discovering ways to reach and restore the confidence and happiness of severely traumatized dogs. Because of her effective rehabilitation methods, she was able to successfully place in homes 100 percent of the dogs she rescued, both on her own and through the Pet Assistance League. Her volunteer obedience training work in animal shelters has been invaluable in making shelter dogs more adoptable. This busy woman is listed in the 26th edition of *Who's Who in the West* and Strathmore's *Who's Who 1999 - 2000.*

Judy now devotes most of her time to teaching people how to develop a communication partnership with their dogs. She teaches seminars through the Colorado Free University for all people wanting to better understand dog behavior, in order to help their own dogs, or just to enjoy dogs more. In her spacious indoor training facility at her ranch, she has solved behavior problems for dogs and their families from throughout the country with a 100 percent success rate. As long as there are dogs suffering and needlessly dying, Judy will continue to promote the lifesaving dialogue between dogs and their owners which dogs need and deserve.

Judy Moore provides canine behavior consulting and personal instruction to dog owners. Requests for seminars, clinics, and individual training should be directed to her at the address below or by e-mail through her web site at http//www.helpyourdog.com.

Judy Moore
Wapiti Run Dog Obedience School
17900 Vista Drive
Buena Vista CO 81211

Acknowledgments

If I were to thank all those dogs which have made plain to me the concepts I have included in this book, I would have to go back to Lassie, a little Pomeranian/Fox Terrier mix which shared my childhood with me. She had been abused and was frightened, and as a child I learned to always be wary and careful, as she might snap unexpectedly at any moment. She was my child-heart's soul-mate. I wanted to help her with her fears, but I did not know how. In large part because of her, I have spent my lifetime learning how.

My many students over the years, both dog and human, provided me a testing ground. I thank all of them for helping me swim upstream against so many wrongly held notions about dog behavior rushing down from the heights of long-accepted dog training.

The wonderful, dedicated people at The MaxFund Animal Adoption Center let me initiate dialogue with many of their canine residents. Thank you for the opportunity to experience dialogue in action with those homeless hounds.

The ArkValley Humane Society gave me a year's worth of society's throwaways to rehabilitate using WR-DOS. I am grateful I had that opportunity.

Thanks to Greg Phillips, Judy Kratky, Karen Hicks, Fred Swart, Jackie Whiteleather, Jeri Swann, Bill Spaulding, Jeremy Moore, Fay Golson, and all their dogs for willingness to be photographed.

Thanks to my family who not only held up under the stress of the book-writing adventure, but who picked me up when I faltered. And to Ampy for feeding us like family.

Special thanks to those who took time to read and comment on what I was writing, to let me know if I was translating the message clearly from the dogs to the public. Thanks Patty, Judith, Doug, and Jeanne.

Words fail me to sufficiently thank Stacy Martin and Aaron Moore of Barking Dog Communications for their willingness to pitch in with their computers and expertise in type and image-setting and graphic design on a moment's notice.

And to Jim, my dedicated editor, illustrator, photographer, farmhand, best friend, and husband, and the one who debated every concept with me until it really crystallized in my thought—my forever gratitude and unending love.

This book is dedicated to the
millions of dogs now in shelters,
waiting and hoping for another chance at life.

Table of Contents

About the Author
Acknowledgments
Table of Contents
Foreword
Preface
Introduction
"A Pastoral Tragedy"   by Thomas Hardy

SECTION I: TOWARD GREATER UNDERSTANDING

CHAPTER 1
Obedient From Birth 19
   An obligation 30
   Foundation stones 31

CHAPTER 2
Dialogue Not Domination 34
   A Language for living 34
   WR-DOS 46

CHAPTER 3
Understanding Behavior 50
   Attentiveness 50
   Response-ability 53
   Emotional stability 55
   Emotional IQ 61

CHAPTER 4
Ensuring Successful Dialogue 65
   Conversation the key ingredient .65
   Accessing WR-DOS 70
   Practice with precision 73
   Laugh as you learn 77
   A new leash on life 78

SECTION II MAKING IT HAPPEN

CHAPTER 5
Attention Please! 83

CHAPTER 6
Side by Side Forever (Heel on and off leash) 96

CHAPTER 7
Alert But Still, Calm, Confident (Sit-stay) 105

CHAPTER 8
Down, But Not Out (Down and Down-stay) 113

CHAPTER 9
Statue-like (Stand and Stand-stay) 125

CHAPTER 10
Come to Me (Recall) 133

SECTION III: SEEING THE BIGGER PICTURE

CHAPTER 11
Moral Commitment 145

CHAPTER 12
For a Better World 149

Afterword 155

Appendix A: Why "Pack Behavior" Is Irrelevant 156

Appendix B: Solutions to Five Specific Problems 158

Appendix C: Student Comments 166

Appendix D: An Amusing Account 169

Appendix E: Wolf Hybrids as Companion Dogs 175

Appendix F: Rescue Organizations 178

Appendix G: Recommended Reading .180

Index 183

Foreword

As I write this, my puppy Oscar and I have been training with Judy for about a week. The progress has been remarkable in that short span of time. Although far from perfect (I know that will come later), he gives me his full attention when his name is called and asks what to do next. For a five-month-old puppy, this is quite an accomplishment.

I have owned dogs since childhood and have bred and shown dogs for 25 years. I feel my previous experience with obedience training was one of power and submission, a disservice to the wonderful dogs I have been privileged to have in my life. Judy has broken the barrier of miscommunication between man and dog. She knows their language and trains them with methods that allow for mutual respect. It is a lesson from which we can all benefit.

Fay Golson
Dallas, Texas

Preface

For many years my dog-owner students have been urging me to write down for their reference all the concepts and procedures I have taught them for changing a timid, or unruly, or aggressive dog into a calm, confident canine partner. I was finally able to respond to their requests, and this book is the result.

My concepts and procedures have been molded by the many dogs I have helped over nearly 40 years. So the book has its roots in my past. I have had a life-long love affair with animals, especially dogs and horses. I began learning to train dogs for obedience work as a teenager in a 4-H program. My partner in the adventure of learning dog obedience training was an overly enthusiastic Springer Spaniel/Saint Bernard mix (picture a black and white Golden Retriever). Together we took top honors in state-level 4-H dog obedience trials.

I am sure the training method I learned in 4-H would approximate most traditional dog training practiced today. But my training methods of my childhood years look crude and clumsy from my present perspective. However, even at that tender age I always instinctively avoided any technique that interfered with the exuberant joy and boundless love my dog expressed. In the years following my 4-H experience, I remained interested in animal behavior, earning my undergraduate degree in zoology.

As I matured, my interest in dog training became a passion. Through books and direct observation, I explored many training methods. But most importantly, I watched and listened to the hundreds of abandoned and/or traumatized dogs I have rescued and rehabilitated. Via their responses to my various forms of interaction with them, these dogs made absolutely clear to me what comprises for them effective communication. What I learned from them has challenged not only the methods but the premises of the other dog training methods I am aware of. Over all these years the dogs have taught me a simple and precise "language" that both the dogs and their owners can quickly learn. That common language between dog and owner makes possible a dialogue that brings harmony, consistency, joy, and an unbreakable bond of love to a lifetime partnership.

Because I know without reservation that the outcome for both dog and owner will be sheer delight, I get excited every single time I train a new dog. The immediacy of every new dog's response is truly awesome. What the dogs have taught me works without fail!

One of the most important and revolutionary differences between my method and traditional training is so simple that it at first sounds insignificant. This revolutionary difference lies in *who speaks first* in the dialogue between dog and owner. Traditional training teaches that the owner speaks first and the dog responds. In my method, the dog must speak first, asking the crucial first question. Though I explain the importance of this concept in this book, it is unlikely you will grasp its full significance until you initiate the dialogue with your own dog. Words alone are inadequate to impress upon you the difference between the dog seeking help/advice from his owner and receiving it clearly, and the dog being ordered to do something. If you learn little else from this book, learn this one thing! You must establish a lifelong dialogue in which the dog asks questions and you provide answers, rather than a communication in which you give orders to the dog.

The supportive relationship between dog and owner which the dialogue fosters enables the dog to develop emotional stability, confidence, self-esteem, and peace of mind. Through the unique method of communication I explain in this book, I have been able to rehabilitate and redeem all kinds of dogs, no matter how severe the behavioral problems seemed to be.

There's a second difference between my training method and traditional training. But it is more important for the owner than for the dog. The difference is this: Most of the training methods I have encountered over the years are easy on the owner but hard on the dogs. By that I mean the dogs are expected to do all the learning while the owner is asked to learn little. The dogs, from whom I learned, did not recommend that approach! In my training method you will employ a language that is very easy for the dog to learn. After two brief sessions, the dog has no more procedures to learn. He only needs practice.

Much more is required of the owner. With my approach, training yourself, the owner, will be 95 percent of your job. The owner must overcome a multitude of preconceptions, attitudes, and physical reactions toward the dog that interfere with clear communication. The new language itself is not difficult for the owner to learn. The owner's challenge is to take seriously the responsibility to become utterly consistent in his use of the language, so that he does nothing to destroy the dog's confidence. I always trust that the enormous benefits for both owner and dog will motivate the owner to replace his urge to dominate his dog with a desire for lifelong dialogue.

The dogs, both those homeless and those cherished, have provided the substance for this book, and I share some of their remarkable stories in its pages. It has been a joy to work with so many dedicated, caring dog owners. The dogs, their owners, and I hope this book will guide you to improve the experience of the dogs in your life and to improve your life with your dog.

NOTE:

Since I am of the opinion that no one really has the right to "own" another living being, but rather to share life with others for mutual benefit, I prefer not to use the term "owner" except for matters of convenience. In this book I interchangeably use the terms "human partner," "handler," and "owner." The important point is that this person, however we reference him, is the dog's essential source of information for how to live happily and safely in a human world.

In attempting to appear unbiased in referring to a dog, I could use "his/her" throughout the book, or I could alternate use of "his" and "her." I have chosen instead for convenience to use the male pronoun consistently without any intent to slight the female gender. As a matter of fact, both of my beloved dogs are females.

Introduction

Have you ever met a bad dog? You may think you have, and I don't blame you. Dogs do all kinds of things—destructive things, aggressive things, annoying things—that are very disturbing to people. And when you think you *have* a bad dog yourself, then you really feel in a bind. Probably, in spite of the bad behavior, you have found a great deal in your dog to love (ever see the movie "Turner and Hooch"?) So you try dog obedience classes or dog obedience trainers. You read dog training books, you watch dog training video tapes, and you catch every dog training special that hits public television. You are always hoping to find some method that will turn your bad dog into a good dog.

Well, my training does not turn a bad dog into a good dog. Wait! Stop! Don't throw this book away. My training does not turn a bad dog into a good dog because in over forty years of working with all kinds of canines, I have never met a bad dog. But I have met more than a thousand dogs who needed my help to prove just how good they really were. Within a very short time after they had met me, I had removed the dust—or caked-on mud—that was hiding their true colors as wonderfully good dogs. I had to brush away some ignorance, confusion, frustration, and fear and give them a way to get the information they needed in order to know how they were expected to behave in a human world. When for the first time in their lives they learned how they were expected to behave, their natural goodness shone through for everyone to see. Not only did they exhibit good behavior, but they became confident and happy. Since you love your dog, you certainly want him to be happy as well as good. My training is fun, incredibly quick, permanent, and effective. And that will make *you* happy.

Let me introduce you to one of those thousand or so dogs:

Mikey is an Australian Shepherd who has been loved dearly by his owner for the entire six years of his life. But many people who lived around Mikey considered him to be a bad dog. He was so aggressive toward people who would get near his car when he was in it that he would try to reach through the window to snap at the arm of a toll booth attendant. If someone moved across a room when Mikey was there, he would often run after the person and snap, sometimes tearing clothing. Despite his aggressive appearance, Mikey was so timid he avoided all strangers whenever he could. Out of love for Mikey, his owner moved to a large acreage outside her city where Mikey could live without having to encounter people. But Mikey wasn't happy.

I met Mikey one evening when the owner came to me seeking a solution to Mikey's problems. I spent an hour or so that evening with both Mikey and his owner, teaching them both what they needed to learn. We worked together again for another half hour the next morning. At that point, a friend of mine, but a stranger to Mikey, was able to run around Mikey while clapping his hands and then approach Mikey and pet him. Mikey calmly accepted the petting with poise and a measure of self-assurance. A short time later, I sat in Mikey's car with him while this stranger approached the car and even rapped on the windows. Mikey sat quietly in the back seat. I spent another hour or so that afternoon teaching the owner how to continue building on the progress Mikey had already made.

By that evening Mikey headed for home with his owner. He was a changed dog—a happy dog who that afternoon had stretched out peacefully full length on his side as we talked near him. Mikey's owner said he had rarely been confident and peaceful enough to assume that position. In my time with Mikey, I had never used a scolding word or a punishing gesture. I worked from the basis of my conviction that Mikey is and always had been a very good dog, and of course no one needs to punish a good dog. One of the owner's friends back home is still talking about "the miracle of Mikey."

Before leaving my ranch that evening Mikey's owner had said to me, "Judy, I don't think you know what you have here." I think I do know, and I'm sharing it with you in this book. Read this book through. Then reread the section on how to do the exercises with your dog. Then study again the instructions for each exercise. Take them one at a time and practice the procedures by yourself, without your dog. Only then should you call your dog to you and show him what you have learned. The effort is worth it. That "bad" dog you love so much will finally become for you the good dog he has always been. You will be amazed and pleased to discover he is just the kind of dog you can happily share your life with.

If you do not yet have a dog, but you think you would like to have one, this book is for you, too. You can use the book in the same way I suggested for dog owners. But I have a very important further suggestion for you. When you are ready to show a dog what you have learned from this book, go to the nearest animal shelter and adopt the dog that most appeals to you. Don't worry if someone warns you that any dog you pick from an animal shelter may turn out to be a "problem dog." If you diligently adhere to the rules and follow the procedures you are taught in this book, the dog you pick will not have behavior problems. Share with that dog what you have learned, and you will also have a good dog to happily share your life with. My experience has shown me that it does not matter where that dog came from or what he has done in his past. This book will help you rewrite that dog's history.

If, as you read this book, you find yourself pondering some new ideas about interacting with other people, you will be joining many of my students in that pondering. I hope you will do just that. What I am learning from the dogs, and what my students are learning from the dogs, may make this a better world for all of us who share the planet. Apply what *you* discover to your relationships with children, the elderly, your colleagues, friends, and family members. See what happens!

"A Pastoral Tragedy"

(excerpted from *Far From the Madding Crowd* by Thomas Hardy)

"Gabriel had two dogs. George, the elder,...though old, he was clever and trustworthy still. The young dog, George's son,...was learning the sheep-keeping business....If sent behind the flock to help them on he did it so thoroughly that he would have chased them across the whole county with the greatest pleasure if not called off, or reminded when to stop by the example of old George....

One night,...Farmer Oak called as usual to the dogs, previously to shutting them up in the outhouse till next morning. Only one responded—old George; the other could not be found....Gabriel then remembered that he had left the two dogs on the hill eating a dead lamb...and concluding that the young one had not finished his meal he went indoors to the luxury of a bed....

It was a still, moist night. Just before dawn he was assisted in waking by the abnormal reverberation of familiar music...the note of the sheep-bell....The experienced ear of Oak knew the sound he now heard to be caused by the running of the flock with great velocity....

He went to the hedge; a gap had been broken through it, and in the gap were the footprints of the sheep...He passed through the trees and along the ridge of the hill. On the extreme summit, where the ends of the two converging hedges...were stopped short by meeting the brow of the chalk-pit, he saw the younger dog standing against the sky—dark and motionless as Napoleon at St. Helena.

A horrible conviction darted through Oak. With a sensation of bodily faintness he advanced: at one point the rails were broken through, and there he saw the footprints of the ewes. The dog came up, licked his hand, and made signs implying that he expected some great reward for signal services rendered. Oak looked over the precipice. The ewes lay dead and dying at its foot....

As far as could be learnt it appeared that the poor young dog, still under the impression that since he was kept for running after sheep, the more he ran after them the better, had at the end of his meal off the dead lamb…collected all the ewes into a corner, driven the timid creatures through the hedge, across the upper field, and by main force of worrying had given them momentum enough to break down a portion of the rotten railing, and so hurled them over the edge.

George's son had done his work so thoroughly that he was considered too good a workman to live, and was, in fact, taken and tragically shot at twelve o'clock that same day…."

Tippy: Rehabilitated through dialogue

SECTION I

TOWARD GREATER UNDERSTANDING

PHOTO MOMENT

No "control" problems here

CHAPTER 1

Obedient From Birth

"All discord, harmony not understood."

Alexander Pope

Dog obedience. Two words that imply much about the way humans view canines. Many people equate "obedience" with "goodness" and "discipline," attributes which dog owners often fail to find in their dogs.

What does obedience really mean? Obedience, according to Webster, is "submission to authority." Dog obedience then means canine submission to authority. In discussions of dogs and their obedience or lack of it, what we fail to recognize is that dogs are born already obedient to an authority. What is that authority? Their instincts! Those instincts would serve them well in a dog world. But the problem is that dogs do not live in a dog world. They live in a human world.

We must face the fact that in order for dogs to survive (not to mention thrive) in a human world, they must obey human authority. So dog obedience training means training a dog to submit to human (most likely his owner's) authority. There is not necessarily anything wrong with this concept if a right mental attitude on the part of the human or humans involved prevails. However, this idea of human authority may subject the dog to the abuses of human ego or to mistreatment through human ignorance. Human ego can stretch the meaning of authority to the point of dominance, even cruel domination. So the right attitude toward dog training has to be established before any training begins.

A right attitude requires a right understanding of the purpose of submission on the part of the dog. The objective in dog training should not be merely to gain control of subordinate beings whose non-human behavior we find irritating and disruptive at times. And certainly dog training must not be an ego-trip for some less-than-noble human character—an opportunity for some insecure human personality to finally fulfill its frustrated desire for dominance and tyranny.

The real purpose of dog training ought to be to make the dog's *instincts*, not so much the dog himself, submissive to human authority. What I mean by that is, in simple terms, the goal of training should be *to enable the dog to override his instincts with response to his owner*. Luckily for us, dogs have one instinct which they can safely obey and which we can use to help us to achieve this goal. This one instinct is the dog's overriding natural desire to communicate with humans.

However, dogs cannot communicate with their owners while their other instincts are commanding all of their attention. Unfortunately, most canine instincts disrupt or interfere with dog-human communication. Dogs are born with one language only—the language spoken to them "from within," from their instincts. These instincts, which vary somewhat from one breed to another, speak to the dog very loudly. Another way to look at it is to consider that dogs are born with a "rule book" for life—for dog life, not life in a human society. A dog consults his rule book when he has questions about what to do in a given situation, but this rule book gives nearly all the *wrong answers* for life in human society!

When dogs are responding to their instinctive language, the dangerously flawed rule book, they are not being "bad" dogs, although their behavior within human society may indeed seem bad. They are actually being very good dogs. The shepherding breed of dog is, in fact, being a very good dog of his breed when he chases cars, or children running, or bikers pedaling past. He's doing, to the best of his ability, what his inbred instincts impel him to do. He only wants to stop what he perceives to be "uncontrolled behavior" and cause the moving car/child/bike to stop stampeding and stand quietly and be attentive to him, the shepherd! But his rightful, instinctive impulse to bring order and discipline to a herd can very well be deadly for him. The car may run over him. His nipping the heels of children may land him in court on an assault charge. It is common knowledge that most court sentences pronounced on dogs who appear to be "aggressive" toward humans are not customarily intended to rehabilitate, but rather to *eliminate*. A recent national television program spotlighted dog attacks on humans. One owner whose dog was found guilty of "aggressive" behavior had to spend $100,000 in legal defense fees to avert destruction of the dog.

For many dogs, behavior in response to the demands of their instinctive language brings a lifetime of criticism and condemnation. It seems that dogs are always in trouble because their rule book gives them all the wrong information for how to behave. The dog is yelled at, smacked around, and repeatedly told how bad he is for doing something he has been preprogrammed, through many generations, to do. Such punishing methods of "training" don't solve the problem because they don't really even address the problem. They only destroy the dog's self-confidence and joy in life. As the dog matures, he becomes increasingly frustrated and insecure. By the time he's two or three years old, he not only has all the wrong information for how to behave, but he has an enormous burden of anxiety, confusion, even anger, from misguided attempts by humans to alter his behavior through scolding, punishment and correction.

Even dogs who have come into reasonably amicable accord with their owners usually live with the stress of confusion. The confusion results from the frustrating conflicts between the nagging demands of their instincts and the incomprehensible restraints and requirements placed upon them by their human owners. The following account by the owner of a very troubled Rottweiler illustrates this point:

> Rajah is a female Rottweiler who has been with us from birth. I'd never been concerned in the least bit for her happiness. I assumed that she was as content and happy as any dog could possibly be. She has three girls to look after, she never has to stay outside, she gets bones, chew toys, rides in the car, trips to the creek, etc. on a regular basis. What's not to be happy about? But for a long time she wasn't. The sad thing was—I didn't even know it.

Rajah always seemed to be very shy. Sometimes you would have thought that she was abused because of the way she would cower and show submission when she was told to do something (we hadn't learned actual commands). I assumed she was showing that she recognized us as the leaders of her pack.

Rajah was always a very playful pup. She was very loving and always very conscious of the little children.

She played very gently with the kids. I don't think she even knew that she was capable of intimidating anyone until....Around the time Rajah turned three, she started acting differently around strangers. She would often snap at anyone who came into the house. I thought of it as a protective trait. There didn't seem to be any rhyme or reason to her selection of victims. She would sniff anyone who came into the house, and if they tried to touch her, she would usually snap at them. Luckily, everyone she snapped at was quick! If visitors ignored her and didn't try to touch her, she would usually be fine with them.

One fine spring day Rajah was in the front yard, off leash. She was so well-behaved in the yard that she never needed to be on the leash, or so we thought. The children were playing with the neighbor kids when a little boy from across the street decided to come play, his grandmother frantically in pursuit. When the little boy arrived in our yard, the grandmother finally caught up with him. When Grandma grabbed the boy, Rajah grabbed Grandma. It wasn't pretty. Luckily Grandma wasn't upset, but I was. However, I rationalized the incident as being evidence of Rajah's protective trait once again.

In order to solve the problem, we vowed to never let

Rajah outside the fenced backyard unless she was on leash. Sounded good anyway. Needless to say, with three children under the age of 12, the gate was left open one unforgettable evening when a young boy was riding by on his bicycle. At that moment Rajah just happened to be wandering through the open gate. She chased the boy down, grabbed him by the ankle, and proceeded to try to get him off the bike.

For me, this was the straw that broke the camel's back. I was torn. Must I put the dog to sleep (I won't have a dog that attacks poor, innocent children), or do I have any other options, I asked myself. In desperation, I searched my phone book for names of trainers. I was seeking advice, but I was pretty sure what I was going to hear. Years before, Rajah's mother had problems with viciously barking while running the fence and chasing anyone who walked by the house. I had contacted a trainer in the area where I was living. She advised me to put the dog down immediately, and she absolutely refused to work with her. Based only on what I explained to her over the phone, sight unseen she diagnosed our dog as "dominant aggressive." Needless to say, I was very disappointed with her advice. So, even as I searched the phone book this time, I knew I was leery of "dog trainers."

The first number I called that day was for Wapiti Run. I am so glad that Judy Moore had her ad in the Yellow Pages. I told Judy our problems, and she immediately gave me hope. Actually, what she said was, "It's not a problem." She shared with me some of her many success stories with dogs, many of whom I have since met, whose problems were far worse than Rajah's. She wanted to start working with us immediately. When I had picked up the phone to begin calling, I had expected to hear, "Put the dog to sleep before she costs you everything you have." By the time I hung up the phone after talking to Judy, I had a much deeper understanding of Rajah's behavior and more hope than I could ever have imagined.

Judy started us the next night. We had five one-on-one sessions. During the first session, Judy assessed that Rajah was incredibly sensitive but had very little, if any, self-confidence, and hardly any self-esteem. This explained so much to me. As we started our training, Rajah and I, I began to learn so much about my dog. I have learned that Rajah's cowering and submissive behavior was caused by her lack of confidence and her not knowing what was expected of her. She hasn't cowered one time since the first night of training. The snapping took more time. When Rajah is faced with a new person, dog, etc., who expresses uncertain energy, because she lacks confidence, she reacts in the only manner she knows—aggressively. But after 3-1/2 months of practicing the routine response exercises, and without my addressing the snapping problem specifically at all, for the first time in her life she was able to allow men to walk into her yard without behaving aggressively.

As we continued in our work together, I began to learn so much about myself. I have also learned how sensitive Rajah is to my moods and feelings. The worst night I had in the group class was a night when I was at my wit's end. I had had a bad day at work. I was irritable at home. Rajah was very in tune—she reacted the same way at class that night! In class, if I have any uncertain energy toward a dog in class, Rajah never fails to want to be aggressive toward that dog. So I have had to learn to control my feelings so that she can learn to control hers. It is all a process. I have learned that all Rajah ever wanted to do was please us, her family. She just didn't know how. It is our job, as her family, to show her how. Judy's job in helping dogs and owners isn't to train the dog so much as it is to teach the human how to help the dog know what is expected and wanted.

I have watched a dog whom I was unable to take on a walk because she would literally drag me down the street become a dog that my two-year-old can walk on a leash. I've witnessed a dog who would chase a bicyclist any chance she got become a dog who can hold a sit-stay in the middle of the street while all the kids in the neighborhood ride in circles around her. I've seen a dog who would cower if someone so much as looked at her crossly become a dog who is happy and content, no longer intimidated by her environment.

I am very proud of our accomplishments. I have learned so much about human behavior in learning how to work with my dog. I have learned how powerful the

influence of human energy is, and I've learned how to
overcome and control fear.   I have learned that
communication has no boundaries.

There is a very alarming trend in the United States right now
which is receiving considerable media attention. Aggression
problems with dogs are becoming more common as more and more
people crowd into diminishing space in this country, providing
more opportunity for unpleasant encounters between dogs and
people. Some people even keep aggressive-appearing dogs, often
large dogs, as a kind of security system.

Accompanying this trend is the ominous statistic that dog bites
are the number one source of injuries to children. Because people
do not understand what is needed to reduce the unpleasant
encounters, wrong steps will be taken to control the problem. Dog
owners will find themselves more and more restricted in what they
can do with their canine companions and where they can do it.
Inevitably, many dogs will even be destroyed. It is imperative that
we solve this problem, like any other, through first gaining an
understanding of what is really going on.

The real solution to this problem will come from understanding
and eliminating the source of a dog's frustration and confusion.
Being told he is bad for doing what he thinks is good, that is, what
his instincts impel him to do, frustrates and confuses the dog. In
most cases the dog's instincts are providing him with the wrong
information because those instincts evolved to make him do well a
job that is no longer relevant to the human society in which the dog
lives.

What the dog needs, we might view as "job retraining." We
should accept the responsibility for giving the dog new
"employment"—activity which fits his job description of "human
companion and comfort" rather than hunter or shepherd. In some
instances the dog may still be needed by his owner to perform the
specific functions for which his breed is distinctly adapted. In such
cases the new job training does not impair the dog's ability. He can
still perform beautifully, but at the request of his owner, not on
automatic pilot.

In order for the dog to understand the requirements of his new "job," the owner must be able to communicate clearly what is expected of him. The new requirements and restraints must fall within the context of completely consistent rules of behavior that the dog can learn and practice throughout his life. That means the dog's instinctive language must be replaced by a second language which is understood in common by both the owner and dog.

The dog's owner must recognize this need and want to meet the need for his dog. He must see how important it is to give his dog this second language which can eventually speak to him more imperatively than his inborn instinctive language.

To be willing to provide the dog with this second language, the owner must want to communicate, not dominate. When a dog is being dominated by a human, he is not being respected for what he is—a companion animal wanting to love, to share, to serve. Loving service and companionship thrive in an atmosphere of clear communication and mutual respect, not in one of domination.

Given the choice, we humans will choose to serve because we love. We don't choose to serve out of fear. Given the opportunity, dogs will do the same. Domination invariably involves some degree of fear. Fear and punishment have no place in the dog's learning. Serving, for man or dog, must spring out of a sense that we have freedom to be our loving selves, not out of fear—fear resulting from domination and slavery.

Clear communication that fosters mutual love and respect cannot prosper in a relationship where *either* party dominates the other. When there is no proper communication between dog and owner, some owners will simply allow the dog to do whatever the dog's impulses dictate. An owner cannot allow the *dog* to rule the roost either! The dog only attempts to assume a dominant role when there is no proper communication between owner and dog.

Unfortunately, many dog training methods minimize the importance of proper communication and place far too much emphasis on this whole issue of who is in a dominant role, the human or the dog. Many trainers espouse a "pack behavior method" of controlling a dog in which the owner asserts his dominance over the dog in the same manner as a canine pack leader. In my experience, teaching the dog that his rank is subordinate to that of his owner (human domination) is not the best way to overcome dominating behavior by a dog. If a dog is influenced by an instinctive impulse toward establishing his dominant place in a pack, that instinct is no more beneficial to the dog in a human society than many of his other instincts. As I've already explained, the dog must learn to subordinate his instincts to his communication with his owner. When his instincts become subordinate, pack behavior becomes as irrelevant as the dog's many other instinctive impulses. (Please refer to Appendix B for further discussion of pack behavior.)

In any case pack behavior methods do not address what I have found to be the dog's real problem. A dog's off-the-wall, unruly behavior, or even aggressive behavior, is not primarily the result of the dog's attempt to assert his dominance. Rather, such behavior results from the chaos and confusion in the dog's mind. Proper owner-dog communication enables the dog to develop conscious self-governance and to subordinate the impulses of his instincts. He learns to stop and ask his owner what is right to do in every situation. That eliminates his mental chaos and confusion.

An owner must recognize how important it is for his dog always to ask what is right to do. To live out his life span in tranquillity and not to be forever on the edge, it is essential that the dog learn that he must not make any decisions without consulting his human partner, asking questions. A dog can only exist in harmony with his owner's human society and live the fullest and happiest life if he can get right answers to his questions about how to behave.

While giving his dog practical answers for living, an owner is also fulfilling the dog's natural desire to companion with and communicate with a human. This is an overriding natural desire for dogs. There are training methods which advocate keeping a dog in solitary, perhaps closed in a bathroom or similar space, for two hours before every training practice session. Then, the proponents of this method explain, the dog will be anxious to practice. What a twisted use of the dog's wonderful natural desire for companionship! If the training method were correct and meeting the needs of the dog, that dog would not need to become desperate for companionship in order to be enthusiastic about a practice session.

In consulting his human partner, asking questions, the dog is asking permission for everything. To act on impulse is *not* asking permission. In acting on impulse, the dog is acting on information from instincts, that faulty rule book. While some impulsive behavior may be quite harmless and, on occasion, even entertaining to man and dog alike, other impulsive behavior is potentially very damaging, even lethal for the dog. No dog can discern which impulsive behavior is benign and which is not! Therefore, he must learn to ask permission about all his actions.

An owner may struggle with requiring his dog to always seek permission—perhaps permission just to run exuberantly after his family's cat. This struggle can result from a misguided sense of love for his dog and a similarly misguided appreciation for his dog's inborn capabilities. The owner may see the requirement for the dog to always "ask first" as too much restraint on the dog's instinctive behavior, even though such behavior jeopardizes the dog's safety.

All dog owners must come to the realization that there is no situation in our present urbanized human society in which a dog can safely be left to respond to his instincts. Dogs are happy, relieved in fact, to trade their independent decision-making for the secure and supportive guidance from their owners. So many dogs I've worked with have within the first few days of training shown an expression that says, "Why didn't you do this for me long ago?"

An obligation

> *"We need another and a wiser and perhaps*
> *more mystical concept of animals....They are not*
> *brethren, they are not underlings; they*
> *are other nations, caught with ourselves in*
> *the net of life and time, fellow prisoners of*
> *the splendour and travail of the earth."*
> Henry Beston, *The Outermost House*

There are many reasons for a person to have a dog in his home and his life. Some reasons are legitimate, some are not. Just as it is wrong for a person to keep a dog in order to have something to dominate and control, so is it wrong to let the dog be the object of a person's desire, for whatever reasons, to cater to every whim of another being. When there is no proper communication between dog and owner, an owner may simply allow the dog to do whatever the dog's impulses dictate. Indulgence (some call it spoiling) is not an acceptable alternative to dominance! Honest love does not promote indulgence. Indulgence, like dominance, does not respect the dog as a companion animal wanting to serve. Only when an owner has consciously worked to develop the kind of communication with his dog which frees his dog from either dominance or indulgence can the owner feel right about having a dog living with him..

We should not keep animals so that we may exploit them. If we keep animals, we should keep them so that we may learn more from them about sharing love. Doesn't communication enhance the expression of love? A relationship between a dog and a human which is one of partnership as well as companionship, demands communication that really works, a language for living. All dogs should be given this language. All dogs deserve to be given a chance to develop their loving potential and live out their lifetimes with certainty, unhampered by emotional instability and uncontrolled inborn impulses which make their lives with humans difficult or even dangerous. Dog and owner must learn to communicate with each other!

Foundation stones

This book introduces a few critical concepts regarding the important interaction and communication between dogs and humans. The dog owner needs to gain an understanding of these fundamental concepts. If he lets these concepts guide his use of formal obedience exercises with his dog as taught in my method, the owner will experience remarkable positive changes in his dog's behavior over an unusually short time span. These concepts are:

Dogs are always being obedient. In other words, they are always obeying the demands of some authority, either their instincts or their human partners.

All dogs are good. We are not going to *make* them good. We are going to enable them to express their goodness in our human society. Humans may frequently think that a dog's behavior is bad, but that doesn't make the dog bad. Therefore, the dog doesn't need to be to told that he's bad. Dogs can be taught all that is required without our ever attacking their self-confidence and self-esteem by scolding and punishing.

Dogs crave a good relationship with man. This inborn tendency of dogs is one of the few which the dog does not need to override and which he can safely respond to. Puppies aren't born with fear or animosity toward humans. No matter how frightened or how aggressive a dog appears to be, he really wants a good relationship with humans. The constant mistakes the dog has made, growing up responding to his inborn rule book and being punished in consequence, prevent the dog from having the good relationship with humans that he craves. Man bears the responsibility for providing the dog with a right way to override the instincts which cause him to make mistakes.

Dogs misbehave for one of two reasons. Either they are *acting on* instincts that violate man's rules; or they are *reacting* negatively to people and circumstances because of anxiety and stress. We condemn dog behavior that we find impulsive and problematic without realizing that this behavior is being prompted, that is, directed or dictated by the dog's instincts. The bad behavior that isn't specifically instinct-driven is the result of the dog's inability to cope adequately with living clueless in a human world. Examples of bad behavior that is instinct driven include *chasing cars, chasing and nipping people, running away, and stealing food.* Examples of bad behavior caused by anxiety and stress include *growling, snapping, and biting, jumping on people, submissive urinating, incessant barking, chewing furniture, compulsive digging, and jumping out of enclosures.* Some trainers prescribe specific procedures, and even drugs, for overcoming each one of these bad behaviors. However, I have found that all these behaviors are adequately diminished or eliminated by establishing the simple communication—between a dog and his human partner—which I advocate in this book.

Dogs must communicate with man by asking questions, and man must provide the answers. Since a dog can't learn all the rules for how to live in a human society, he has to be able to get correct information for how to behave directly from man. To have a safe, secure and harmonious life in human society, a dog must learn not to make any decisions without consulting his human partner, asking questions. The human partner must in turn agree to always respond to the dog's questions with right answers. The dog and his human partner must enter into a consistent and sustained dialogue using a language they share in common.

CHAPTER 2

Dialogue Not Domination

*"Dialogue helps us learn to treat one another with the honor
and respect required for helping us all to feel special."*

From *Dialogue* by Linda Ellinor and Glenna Gerard

A language for living

Imagine, if you will, that you wake up one morning to find that you have been transported into an entirely alien culture—a culture about which you've never heard anything at all. You have brought with you all that you know from your earthly upbringing…let's say a fluency in Romance languages, comfort with the alphanumeric system, great proficiency in calculus, and a Christian heritage. Unfortunately, all that is of no use to you in this new culture in which you find yourself. You do not know the laws of the land, the systems of measurement, the written or the spoken language, the religious taboos, the social conventions, nothing! And nothing of that store of knowledge which you brought with you will tell you any of these things. Furthermore, and perhaps mercifully, no one tells you that certain mistakes can result in instant death.

You will endeavor to survive and have some satisfaction from life, but everything you do will have to be accomplished by trial and error. Not a good recipe for long life; and self-confidence and self-esteem are unimaginable. Mental and physical trauma, if not death, lurk around every corner if you ignorantly make a wrong move.

Wouldn't it be desirable, maybe delightful, even invaluable if you could awake that morning to find your best friend—who just happens to know the culture and the language—right there beside you to interpret everything for you and advise your best course of action moment by moment, for the rest of your life? You might or might not learn details of that culture, but it really will not matter how many of those details you actually learn because your friend has promised to be by your side whenever you venture out into that alien world. You will have great prospects for a long and even joy-filled life, and you can go forward with confidence, peace, and pride in yourself. Such good fortune everyone in this situation should have!

Well, when a dog is born, he essentially awakes into a culture about which he can know nothing. At least by the time he is separated from his mother, he needs that "best friend" to interpret everything for him and advise him about how to make every move. You can and must be that best friend for your dog. You can make it possible for your dog to live successfully in a human culture that is completely alien to him. Because of your help, he will never *have* to learn all the rules of that culture. You know all those rules. Since you are partnered with your dog for life and are his best friend, *you* can interpret the world for him and advise him.

Certainly that constant interaction between you and your dog will make the living of your partnered lifetime together more interesting and enjoyable. It creates a relationship, a bond, between you and your dog that far exceeds the expectations of most dog owners. But if you're going to be your dog's lifelong interpreter and advisor, you must first have a language in common with your dog, a language that you both understand.

I have developed a simple language that makes interaction between a dog and his owner easy and enjoyable for both. This language allows me to quickly establish a dialogue, a two-way communication, in which the dog speaks first, asking what to do, and a human provides reassuring, practical answers. The all-important key to the unusual effectiveness of the dialogue this language makes possible is that *the dog is allowed to speak first*, asking a question. The dog may not always be first to speak, but the opportunity must always be there for him to do so. He will take good advantage of that opportunity. Once the dog knows how to ask his questions, he will never again be forced to make decisions based on his flawed inborn rule book because his human best friend can give him answers to guide him in making safe and appropriate decisions.

Of course, the dog must first learn to ask his questions and begin the dialogue. To induce the dog to ask the first question, his human partner sets up a circumstance or situation in which the dog *must* repeatedly make a decision (see Chapter 5 for execution). Since the dog does not yet know how to ask for information from a human, he will have to make that repeated decision based on an inborn directive, an instinct. The instinct which will aid him is the one instinct that he can safely listen to: his powerful desire to companion with man. Thank goodness for this instinct! It is the cornerstone upon which the entire structure of the dialogue is built.

Because of the circumstance that his handler has set up, the dog must turn to his human partner and ask for information. I call this moment when the dog turns to his human companion and asks the first question the "initiation of dialogue." Because of the urgency of the decision he's making, the dog reaches this initiation of dialogue very quickly, often in as little as one minute! An owner tells how Sizzle, an energetic Sheltie, enjoyed her experience:

> Having found an earlier obedience course an unproductive chore, my dog and I discovered the "Moore Method" to be amazingly effective – and we're having fun too! For us, the exercise that positions the whole process seems to be the very first one – "free walking" with quick 180-degree turns by the human partner. My dog immediately understood that she must watch alertly. Since literally the first minutes of this training, she has been enthusiastically attentive. Thank goodness we have no more leash yanking, the standard "method of operation" in our previous course.

The dog's attentiveness to his partner is engendered by the simple fact that this human best friend is extremely important to him. Remember, you as your dog's human partner are your dog's best friend. You and your dog have a partnership relationship requiring dialogue, not a master/servant relationship based on unilateral demands. The dog brings to your relationship love, a desire for companionship, and his questions. You also bring love and a desire for companionship. And you bring answers. The two common elements—love and a desire for companionship—form the glue that bonds man to dog. In the dialogue, that glue is strengthened by the answers that you give to the dog's questions because your answers always bring the dog harmony. Obviously, you always have the responsibility to be ready to give your partner only correct advice and to demand of your partner only what is fair and right.

When I initiate a dog's training, I am the first human partner he dialogues with (even though I may not be his lifetime partner). Once the dog has learned to turn to me and ask what to do, it's very easy for me to teach him simple exercises which will always provide an answer to his all-important question: "What should I do right now?" These exercises form the main components of the all-important dialogue between the dog and myself or another human partner. The exercises I use are those required for AKC Novice Level (**Heel on and off leash**, **Sit**, **Down**, **Stand**, **Sit-Stay**, **Down-Stay**, **Stand-Stay**, and **Come**).

The exercises really provide two things. Each exercise, part of which is a command coming from me, provides the dog with an answer to his question, "What should I do now?" Further, each exercise, as it is executed by the dog, becomes his way to respond to my answer. In this way the dialogue, the two-way communication necessary for the dog's well-being and safety, is completed.

Most people are surprised to find out that after I've achieved the initiation of dialogue, the great majority of the dogs that I work with *appear* to learn the exercises, mostly off leash, within another 15 minutes! In my school there are no "beginning" and "advanced" programs, no 10-step programs. Dialogue makes the training process short and simple.

Now how can virtually all the dogs I work with respond accurately to AKC Novice Level commands in only 15 minutes? One reason for the dog's rapid progress in executing these exercises, the main components of the dialogue, is the precision of the language I've developed for communicating with the dogs. This language consists of three fundamental elements: voice tone, body movements, and energy level, used in various combinations. (The details of the language are explained with the explanation of each exercise in later chapters of this book.)

Understand that while the dogs have not at this stage learned the commands for the exercises, they *do* understand the language that I use. They can understand it because I developed this language over about four decades of studying the responses of thousands of dogs to my voice, body, and energy. Every element of the language is very clear, simple, and precise so that the dog can immediately grasp it. Each combination of body movement, voice tone, and energy level has an obvious and specific meaning for the dogs.

Another reason a dog makes such rapid progress is that I understand that the dog does not and must not be expected to immediately comprehend the command words themselves. In the first sessions, although the dog *appears* to have learned most of the commands for the exercises during that first 15 minutes, he really is just responding naturally to the cues and signals he receives from my very specific and absolutely consistent combinations of voice tone, body movement, and energy level.

The reason my training method for the exercises is so positive and confidence-building for the dog is precisely because I *do not* hold the dog accountable for responding to the command words themselves during that first 15 minutes, or even during the ensuing 15 days or more. Whoever is practicing with the dog will physically assist the dog in executing the exercises (will "make it happen" for him) for as long as is necessary until each exercise becomes a body reflex for him. Sixty or 90 days or even longer is totally acceptable.

Let me illustrate what I do, and why, by giving you another analogy. Suppose you are sitting in a chair next to a table, and there is a glass on the table. A gentleman who speaks only some language you do not know (how about Swahili?) approaches you and addresses you. You look at him questioningly. Suddenly he commands, "Hand me that glass!" Since you haven't a clue as to what he is saying, all you can do is give him another questioning look. He continues repeating the command to you, getting louder and sterner each time: *"HAND ME THAT GLASS!!!!"* Soon your questioning look turns to one of apprehension, and you very much wish that either the gentleman would go away or that you could leave the scene. The man has tried pointing to the glass, so you guess he is referring to the glass, but you cannot be sure what he is saying or what your response should be. You have lost confidence, you are not happy, you have learned no Swahili in the process, and the man does not have the glass. In many dog training methods I have observed, the process and the results are quite similar to what I have just described.

Now suppose instead that this Swahili-speaking gentleman walks up to you with a pleasant expression on his face and in a pleasant tone asks you (commands you) to hand him the glass. As soon as he has said the words, he places your hand around the glass, while smiling reassuringly, lifts your hand and the glass, and transfers the glass to his empty hand. Then he pays you money! Over time, this man will come up to you and do this hundreds of times. Every time he is pleasant and reassuring. He gives the request (as a command so that you do not have the option to decline), he "makes it happen" for you, and he pays you money!

Very soon in this process you begin to look forward to seeing this man and performing this service of handing him the glass because you love being paid. (For the dog, your enthusiastic approval of him and genuine appreciation of him constitute abundant "pay.")

After a while, you begin to recognize the words the man is using, and you no longer require him to "make it happen." But along the way, you were never quizzed on the new language. The entire process of learning some Swahili has been stress-free for you. My method of teaching a dog the language he needs for dialogue is similarly stress-free.

Once the dog learns the language for dialogue (the commands for the exercises), he will be extremely responsive to those words. Be aware of this, and respect him by not using those command words randomly and carelessly in the dog's presence. When I am speaking with another person in the presence of one of my dog students, I always spell every command word. Believe it or not, some dogs have indicated to me that they eventually learned to recognized the spelled commands as well!

I have already made clear the importance of establishing dialogue and using precise, consistent language to make the dog's learning quick and stress-free. The foregoing analogy brings out a third reason the dogs respond so quickly to my training method: the dog receives constant and effusive praise for everything he does. Because I'm completely convinced from years of experience that all dogs are doing their best to be obedient to the only rules they know, I regard all the dogs' behavior to be "good" from the dogs' point of view. I make abundantly clear to every new dog I encounter that I believe he is being wonderfully good. I do this by lovingly and enthusiastically praising him from the moment I meet him.

So many training methods employ what is called "positive reinforcement," anything from praise to food treats, to reward the dog for what the trainer or owner judges to be good behavior. And these methods employ negative reinforcement, anything from scolding to electric shock, to discourage behavior the trainer considers to be bad. I have found negative reinforcement, any form of punishment, to be counterproductive. Dogs need to reduce their anxiety, which is itself a major reason for problem behavior. Punishment only adds to their anxiety.

My experience has consistently shown—even with dogs which have severe behavioral problems, such as biting people or destroying property—that what every dog most needs is correct and precise answers to his legitimate and important questions as to *how* to live harmoniously in human society. All the frustration, fear, insecurity, anxiety, "stubbornness," and "impulsiveness" that lead to the most obnoxious or threatening behavioral problems arise from the inability of human owners and trainers to meet this most important need.

Training methods should, as a *first priority*, enable, and more importantly *induce*, the dog to ask his human partner what he should do moment by moment. If trainers fail to recognize the importance of this priority, the training period will likely be protracted (sometimes indefinitely long) and unpleasant. And such training is usually ineffective over the long term. Moreover, the dog has some measure of his joy and enthusiasm for life stolen from him as he submits to human domination.

Following the initiation of dialogue, every dog I work with learns very quickly how to ask his questions. When a dog's human partner knows the language to use to provide the dog with consistent and correct answers, the dog can, for the first time in his life, live in an environment of constant approval and praise. Because the human partner even makes the correct response happen for the dog, the dog lives in the confidence of being always right, always pleasing his owner (see explanations of the exercises in Section II). Frustration, insecurity, fear, anxiety, and "impulsiveness" melt away and with them the mild or severe behavioral problems that they caused. The dog and his human partner live in a constant friendly dialogue, wherein the human can always give the dog a positive answer to his questions.

Training methods, though well-intentioned, that fail to meet this most basic need of every dog—his need for answers—are actually distressingly misdirected. Some methods employ special equipment—special leashes, head collars, punishing collars, mechanical devices, noise-makers, etc.—to overcome behaviors impelled by the dog's instincts, or faulty rule book. Some methods employ food treats or toys to overcome those same instinctive dog behaviors.

The way to a dog's mind is *not* through his stomach or his muscles and nerves. Furthermore, how much can a food treat or toy satisfy the dog's yearning to have answers to his questions? Every dog really needs to know how to please his owner, how to live harmoniously with other people and other dogs, how to turn from his faulty inborn rule book to a new source of direction for his actions, how to rid himself of the anxiety and frustration of conflicting priorities and motivations. And woe be to the dog's owner if a crisis occurs at a moment when gimmicks and treats are not available but are still required to elicit response. For these reasons, I use no treats or gimmicks. The way to a dog's mind is not through his stomach, it is through his mind and his heart, through his natural ability to interact intelligently and lovingly through *language*.

Here's how two students felt about my method:

Kodiak, our Golden Retriever, was eight years old, and Keesha, our Black Lab, was eight months old when

we took them to Judy Moore for training. We were most impressed with Judy's positive approach in her training techniques. Using nothing but positive feedback and a quick correcting tone, we were amazed at how quickly the dogs' behaviors were modified.

Most importantly, the dogs thoroughly enjoyed every session, as did we! By consistently following Judy's training technique, we've noticed continued improvement as the dogs mature.

These students told me that over the years with their older dog they had tried many training ideas that they had gleaned from reading lots of books on dog training. Some things, they said, seemed successful at first, but nothing ever worked for very long. This was the first time they had encountered ideas that really worked—permanently.

Dogs need dialogue. It is easy to see how the scolding and punishment usually associated with negative reinforcement can interrupt dialogue, or even make dialogue impossible. Punishment induces fear, and fear discourages the dog from asking his questions.

It is perhaps not as easy to discern how the so-called positive reinforcement of food treats, toys, noise-makers, etc. also interrupt and preclude learning that all-important dialogue. But think about it. The food treat, toy, etc. would turn the dog's attention *away* from his human partner. In a crisis, the dog might be sniffing out the treat and thereby missing the next crucial bit of information coming to him from his owner.

Training methods that fail to meet the dogs' need for dialogue will doubtless continue to be employed because dogs are incredibly loving, forgiving, and resilient. Some dogs just lovingly and peacefully submit to their owners' crude methods of domination. Most dogs grow accustomed to their owners' inconsistencies and lack of communication skills and make the best of the situation. They usually find ways to circumvent or mitigate the effects of inadvertently abusive measures used by owners and trainers.

> **Dogs which make mistakes because of wrong information are not "bad." Neither are misinformed dog owners "bad." If you have made mistakes in past training efforts, you are free to learn and go forward. Do not take a guilt trip because of past mistakes.**

Some dogs even make a game of manipulating their owners and trainers. Less creative dogs or dogs with passive personalities just forgive their owners and resign themselves to a life without luster. But there are some dogs sensitive enough to be traumatized by the unintended abuse that accompanies so many well-intentioned but ill-informed training procedures. These dogs become some of the "problem dogs" that are destroyed by the millions, either by owners or by animal shelters. This loss is so useless and tragic.

Dogs develop problems for many reasons. I am especially grateful I have found the way to reach and rehabilitate the so-called "problem dogs" in our society. Of the hundreds of problem dogs that have been brought to me, every single dog has been rehabilitated. Both the dogs and their owners have been rescued from unnecessary tragedy. Whether trauma is caused by well-intentioned but misguided training methods or by deliberate harassment of the dog, the resultant problem behavior puts the dog's life at risk. Let me tell you about one memorable case of a dog being brought back through my training from the brink of certain disaster:

> An owner called me for advice about her 160-pound Rottweiler. This dog spent his days in the fenced yard of his home while his owner was at work. Only after considerable time had passed did his owner become aware that neighborhood children were harassing this dog by throwing objects at him from the roof of the next-door building. Because of this harassment, the dog was beginning to distrust and resent people. One day a family member came to visit this dog owner, and the Rottweiler was so threatening and aggressive that the family members had to remain in their car. If a dog of that size had similarly threatened a non-family member, court action and destruction would very probably have ensued.
>
> In great fear, the owner asked me if I could help her dog. I didn't assume it would be easy, but I was happy to help. Initiating dialogue with this dog was a great challenge for me because the dog didn't trust me any more than any other human, and he outweighed me by nearly 40 pounds! This was one of the few times when I had to rely on a muzzle to level the playing field a bit. I'll be the first to admit that my first session with that dog was the most physically and mentally challenging session of my career. But like all my dog students, this dog only heard praise and approval from me as I sought to initiate dialogue. And like all my dog students, he responded very quickly and was soon being very attentive and responsive. I worked with him, first initiating dialogue and then beginning the obedience exercises, for about a half hour each of the first two sessions. At the end of the second session when I walked with him back to his car, I asked him to sit beside me and wait for me to open his car door, as I do with every dog. I looked down at him and somehow just knew that I could remove his muzzle, which I did. It was a moment I have not forgotten. He sat there quietly while I petted him and talked with him before I gave him the go-ahead to get into his car.

The next day I began teaching the owner how to dialogue with her dog so she could begin daily practice. After another day had passed, this owner called to share some spectacular news with me. She had been driving down a street with her Rottweiler. As they approached two pedestrians and a bicyclist, she had instinctively braced herself and white-knuckled the steering wheel, expecting the usual aggressive, explosive reaction from her dog. There was no sound. She looked in her rear view mirror and saw the dog just looking calmly out the window at those people as they passed them. The owner has informed me that the change for the dog has been permanent.

> **Dialogue rehabilitates severely traumatized dogs. Imagine how much this communication can help any other dog. All dogs deserve dialogue.**

This puppy learned dialogue at three months old.

Along with the training, the owner also took steps to protect the dog from further harassment by neighbors. There are many occasions when, sadly to say, we have to protect our dogs from ignorant or malicious abuse by unthinking humans. It seems that keeping a dog within his own yard is not always enough. You also have to be able to keep ill-intentioned people away from the dog and his space. Unfortunately, a fenced yard does not guarantee that a dog has an undisturbed space. As we have just seen, a dog can be greatly disturbed by people ignorantly or maliciously throwing objects at him when he is within his yard. Furthermore, many dogs become troubled when people approach their fence barriers. Perhaps being so close to people without being able to comfortably "connect" with them is very frustrating or otherwise upsetting for many dogs. For this reason, I advise dog owners, as a general rule, not to allow people to greet or pet their dogs over or through a fence. It can amount to harassment for a dog that is troubled by a fence barrier. Therefore in some cases a dog may need his own protected space inside his yard's perimeter fence when that fence is accessible to the public.

WR-DOS

Thus far I have discussed my development and use of the language that enables the all-important dialogue. The dog's owner, his lifelong human partner, has the most vital role to play in this dialogue. The owner must dedicate himself to learning to use the exact language that I use. Fortunately the rudiments of the language are simple and can be learned with a little practice. To accommodate the dog's learning process, only one person should work with the dog during the initial training sessions and for a period of a few weeks of practice. It is not fair, in the early stages, to expect the dog to learn the different "dialects" which different human handlers would inevitably introduce into the language. However, once the main components of the dialogue, the AKC Novice Level exercises, are in place for the dog, other handlers can begin working with the dog, provided they adhere to the exact language described in the following chapters of this book.

To illustrate how the exercises can be used by any human handler as a basis for entering into a comfortable dialogue with the dog, provided both the dog and the human know the language, I like to use another analogy that most people can relate to in our computer age. Think of what it takes for a computer to perform successfully the functions that we humans demand of it. The computer has enormous performance potential, but we must be able to access that potential. In order to access the power of the computer, we must install an operating system, typically called a disk operating system, or DOS. Once the operating system is installed, anyone who knows how to use the operating system can access the tremendous performance capabilities of the computer. Similarly, once the basic exercises comprising the dialogue, the dog operating system I teach, are "installed" in the dog, anyone who knows how to access those exercises can enter into a completely successful dialogue with the dog.

Because this analogy has been helpful to my students, I have adopted the acronym WR-DOS to represent my training system. (The WR comes from "Wapiti Run," the name of my horse/dog/rescued-critter ranch in the mountains of central Colorado.) Wapiti Run Dog Operating System. It is a catchy and slightly humorous way to reinforce the important point that this specific system of training, including its language and its dialogue, very quickly becomes a permanent part of the dog's nature.

I have been amazed at just how permanent the "installation" can be. My own dogs have more often than not been rescue cases. One, however, came about in a bizarre way:

> At one point in time, I was asked to both dogsit and train a 6-month-old German Shepherd puppy. I normally will not proceed in this manner because my method is based on developing dialogue between a dog and his owner. However, this particular time I agreed, with the understanding that I would work with the owner when he returned for his puppy. The owner did return for the puppy, but there was no follow-up on the training.
>
> About two years later I encountered this German Shepherd again. She was with a second owner by that time, and it was obvious that she still was in need of a responsible, caring home. I was told that she had never been in a house as she was too hard to control. As far as I could tell, she had spent all of her life up to that point chained to a dog house.
>
> I was able to remove her from that abusive situation and adopt her (we named her Taschen). She had had no socialization and was intimidated by everything. When we arrived home with her, we immediately took her into the house. What about control? Did she tear up our house? No. She remembered what I had "installed" *years* before, and our communication, our dialogue, controlled and guided her and gave her confidence.
>
> Everything inside a house was new to her. As she wandered about the room, timidly investigating each appliance and piece of furniture, this was our dialogue: When she put her nose to an object, I would treat that as

> a question and answer her either with a correcting tone
> (if the object was something she should avoid), or with
> encouraging praise. In that way, in just a few minutes,
> Taschen became a house and hearth dog.

From time to time I have worked with dogs at our local animal shelter, "installing" WR-DOS to release these frightened animals from the frustrations and anxiety their lives have inflicted upon them and to make them happier, more peaceful, and more adoptable. Occasionally one of these dogs has been brought to me for training weeks or even months after leaving the shelter. Usually, of course, the dog has been subjected to differing, and often counterproductive, handling since I "installed" WR-DOS. Though sometimes I did not at first even recognize the dog, as I proceeded into the initial process of building the dialogue, it became immediately obvious that the dog had not forgotten our earlier work together. It was literally as if I'd only worked with the dog the day before. WR-DOS was still there, installed and waiting to be accessed by the owner. The owner only needed to learn the exact language to access all the loving potential of the lifelong dialogue. Furthermore, once WR-DOS is in place, the framework can be fleshed out in an infinite number of ways to match the infinite number of unique living situations in which dogs find themselves.

Replace in your thought the notion that you use AKC Novice level obedience exercises to exert dominance over your dog. Think of these exercises as serving many functions, but *not* domination. Here are just some examples of functions:

- Each exercise becomes a primary means for the dog to respond to his owner. Here is one example of the response function:

  There is a knock at the door. The dog looks to his owner with the question, "What should I do?" The owner answers by giving the dog the command **Sit-stay.** The dog responds by sitting and holding his sitting position until the owner releases him and gives him another directive. The **Sit-stay** exercise gave the dog a way to respond to several possible desires of his owner:

a. being calm and quiet in the presence of a visitor;
b. keeping away from the visitor;
c. not interrupting the conversation or activity of the visitor and his owner.

- The **Sit-stay** exercise can also serve a therapeutic function if the dog has a hyperactive personality and has trouble controlling himself in exciting circumstances. Other exercises may also be used as therapy for dogs with similar difficulties.

- Lastly (in importance to the dog), if someone desires to compete with his or her dog in obedience trials for the CD degree, all exercises used in WR-DOS are the very ones used in obedience competition.

DOWN-STAY was therapy for this easily spooked dog

CHAPTER 3

Understanding Behavior

Attentiveness

Dogs have a sense of smell that is reportedly one to three million times as acute as ours. Try to imagine how the world would impact you if your nose functioned as your dog's does! It is very difficult for a dog to give attention to something with his eyes and ears. His nose predominates! If you are going to dialogue with your dog, his nose has to become subordinated to his eyes and ears. Humans find it difficult to communicate intelligently by using odors! The dog must learn to use his eyes and ears to receive information from his human partner's verbal and body language.

Have you ever noticed that all dogs "walk their owners" when on leash, i.e., lean into the leash and lead the way? Keeping that tactile communication via the collar and leash is the dog's easiest way of knowing where his human walking companion is while he freely pursues all that is assaulting his nose. His leading the way and pulling is only partly due to his being eager to get to wherever he wants to go, and to get there faster than his human escort. He is using the principle demonstrated by the blind person who has a stiff harness connection to his guide dog, enabling him to feel where the dog is at all times. It is very important for the dog to know that his human companion is still with him. Like the blind person, the dog can feel secure, knowing where his human partner is at all times. However, he has no way to ask questions and get answers.

Let's consider another example of tactile reliance. A mother and her toddler are in a crowd watching a parade go by. If the toddler is willing to hold the mother's hand, the mother can enjoy the parade, knowing that the child is securely there beside her.

Now let's translate this scenario to our situation with the dog. For our analogy, the mother represents the dog, and the toddler, the dog's human partner. If the human allows the dog the "stiff connection" (holds his hand) via the leash, the dog has the security he desires of knowing where his human partner is. In the analogy, if the child refuses to hold the parent's hand, the parent will have to check constantly on the whereabouts of the child to assure his safety. If the human partner refuses to "hold the hand" of the dog, i.e., make contact with him via the leash, the dog will have to pay attention to his partner's whereabouts. Just as the parent can grasp the child's hand in his and force the issue, so the dog, by leaning into the leash, attempts to force the issue. But the dog's human partner, by always keeping the leash slack, refuses to let the dog "grasp his hand." Remember, it is very important to the dog to know that his human companion is still with him. But his companion has now deprived him of tactile reliance. By depriving the dog of tactile reliance, the handler has taken the first step toward inducing the dog to ask questions and get answers.

Thus the human has created a circumstance wherein the dog must use his eyes and his ears to keep track of his companion's whereabouts.   He has no other choice! Since there can be no dialogue without constant visual attention from the dog, this means of causing the dog to pay attention with his eyes and his ears is the preparatory step for dialogue. The human partner simply refuses to let the dog know via the leash where he is at any given moment.

It is most interesting to realize just *how* the dog eventually learns to look to his human partner for a directive concerning his every action. This learning takes place in the following manner: First of all, understand that any threat on your part to "not be there" for him—to take away your companionship, to leave without warning—is cause for red flags and multiple alarms in your dog's mind. The dog's human partner can use this fact to gain the dog's undivided attention.

While practicing the simple exercise which teaches the dog to pay attention with eyes and ears (detailed in Chapter 5), the clever owner takes advantage of every potential distraction that appears on his scene as a reason to threaten to "disappear." After his owner "disappears" a few times, the dog begins to get the concept:

"Whenever anything new and interesting appears, I had better double-check where Owner is."

Soon the dog is looking to his human partner whenever he sees something of interest. That provides the human with the perfect opportunity to tell the dog what he can/might/should do about each item of interest at each point in time at each location. For example, it may not always be wrong to give chase to a jackrabbit, but it certainly is always wrong if the rabbit appears on the opposite side of a busy highway! The dog cannot know when chasing a rabbit is an okay idea and when it is not. But if he looks to his human partner every time he spies a rabbit, his partner can indicate to him his best course of action under each circumstance.

Until we have the dog's attention with his eyes and his ears, there can be no dialogue in which the dog speaks first. Without this communication, any attempt at genuine training is essentially futile. Once the dog's attention is gained, after the initiation of dialogue, what appear to be miracles happen in minutes! The following account is from a student who had implemented some kind of obedience training during her time with her four-year-old dog, but was missing that key of attentiveness:

> Before I took River through the training program, he wouldn't pay much attention to me when I gave him commands. He knew how to sit and come, etc., because my husband and I had worked with him some. But most of the time River wouldn't listen to me. The first day that River and I trained with Judy, my husband noticed how much calmer River appeared to be. Since that time I have found that River is much more attentive to me, even in situations where there are other animals around.

And what if a dog does not have both eyes and ears? Either sight or hearing by itself *is* enough and works awesomely for this family:

> We got Tracey from the Humane Society. It was love at first sight. The day I brought her home I knew there was something different about her so I took her to the vet just to be sure. He confirmed my suspicion. Tracey was deaf. I talked to a lot of different professionals, dog

trainers, etc. who all said deaf dogs don't make good pets and she should probably be put to sleep. Not to mention she's a pit bull.

Then I found Judy Moore. With her dog training Tracey understands what she needs to do by hand signals. She's the best pet we could ask for.

Deaf dogs and blind dogs have no need to snap at people out of fear when they have gained peace and confidence through dialogue with their human partners. If they are attentive to their partners and not obliviously following their noses, they will not be startled or frightened by someone's touch.

Response-ability

The exercises that comprise the main components of the dialogue can be life-saving for dogs. But if they are really to save the dog from a life-threatening crisis, the dog must learn to respond to each command with a "body reflex" reaction, not a cerebral response. If someone behind you were to shout, "So-and-so (your name), duck!," quite predictably you would duck your head and then, perhaps, look to see why you were asked to do so. That is because sometime in your past you hit your head soundly when you failed to respond quickly enough to the command, "Duck." You still remember that experience vividly enough that your response to that word is instantaneous. I have already explained that when the dog is learning the exercises, his handler (the dog's owner or other human partner) physically "makes it happen for him." Because a handler puts the dog in each position which a command word requires, and does this many, many times, the dog will develop a reflex response to the command.

Some experts say dogs take as long as 10 seconds to process information such as a command. In a life-threatening situation, that may be too long. That is why the dog must be able to respond with a body reflex action rather than a cerebral response. It is that unquestioning, immediate response that may save his life on more than one occasion.

The dog must also learn that when he hears his name, there is only one acceptable response. When he hears his name, he should respond with, "What?," and that is *all* he should do. He must not jump the gun and attempt to second-guess what his human partner's directive will be. He learns to expect that his name will be followed by a specific directive, and he knows he must listen for that directive. So be sure to say the dog's name before every command.

You will be grateful for this "freeze and ask" response when the day comes that your dog is exploring around on the opposite side of a railroad track from you, and a train comes. If your dog's response to his name is to instantly run to you, the outcome could be disastrous. How much better the outcome will be if he has learned to hear his name, freeze, look at you, and wait for whatever you can communicate to him to keep him out from under that train. This is no hypothetical example I have just given you, as verified by another grateful student:

A remote DOWN can save your dog's life

I have an Australian Shepherd mix who is truly my partner and best friend. It's amazing how much through- o u t each day we use the W R - D O S training. One day that training saved my dog's life. I live near the railroad tracks. On that particular day Wylie did something he's never done before.

He flushed a rabbit and ran right across the tracks after it. On the other side of the tracks he lost the rabbit. He was starting back toward me when I saw a train coming. So I just yelled his name really loudly, got his attention, and gave him the hand signal for "down." He lay right down and waited until the train passed. Then he waited for me to give him the signal to come to me, which he then promptly did. That saved my dog's life. I don't doubt it for a minute.

Emotional stability

Most acts of aggression by dogs, or what we perceive as aggression, are impulsive—that is, prompted, or more likely even dictated, by the dog's faulty inborn rule book. They occur when the dog is not comfortable with whatever is happening around him. Dogs that are timid and insecure are the most likely to be uncomfortable when an unexpected or unfamiliar event occurs. Anything the dog does not understand may constitute a crisis for the dog. Any event, from the arrival of a stranger at the door to the exuberant activities of a group of children, can appear to be frightening or threatening to him. In an attempt to bring a frightening or threatening environment under his own control, a dog employs instinctual behavior which to us appears to be aggressive. Instinctual behavior is the only option for a dog who has not been brought into an effective dialogue with a human partner.

The most effective means of overcoming instinctual aggressive behavior is the elimination of the confusion and frustration that give rise to anxiety and insecurity in a dog. The confusion and frustration can be eliminated by the dialogue between the dog and his human partner. Daily practice of the obedience exercises which are used for dialogue gives the dog a daily boost to his self-esteem. For the first time in his life the dog is experiencing a certainty that he knows what to do to gain consistent approval.

Through comfortable repetition, ten minutes each day, the exercises gradually become automatic body reflexes for him. The dog finds he is calmly responding to his human partner in most circumstances virtually without effort. The repetitive practice of the exercises does for the dog essentially what Toastmasters Clubs do for humans. Such clubs allow humans who are afraid to speak in public to practice speaking among familiar surroundings and before an audience of familiar faces. Frequent repetition in a comfortable setting builds the confidence the speaker needs to face more threatening situations.

Likewise, through practice the dog learns to turn in a crisis to his human partner for direction instead of to instinctual behavior patterns. I have seen high-strung dogs with defensive temperaments which led them to snap at people, or even bite, develop a positive sense about themselves that visibly radiates in the happy expression on their faces. Gone is the impulse to react nervously or bite. Here's a typical happy-ending story:

We bought Klansey, a full-blooded Cocker Spaniel, in February of 1990. My husband had a Cocker Spaniel when he was a little boy, and that was his choice of breeds. Klansey was a well behaved and playful puppy.

In May of 1991 we had our first baby girl. Klansey, the baby and I would go for walks every day.

When our daughter was about 1-1/2 years old, the dog bit her on the face.

They were both eating something while sitting together on the floor. We felt it was our fault to put the child that close to the dog while he was eating. A few years later we had another baby girl. Klansey would bite her on the fingers every now and then when she was trying to feed him. These were more nips than bites until...

One day Klansey and the girls were in the front room by themselves. I heard a loud growl and then a scream. Klansey had bitten our youngest daughter, age 2-1/2, deeply on the face. The child had teeth scratch marks all over her face and a large cut. It took five stitches to close up the cut. That started the opinion wagon. My family, in-laws, friends and relatives all had solutions. Klansey, our six-year-old cocker was an outcast. Almost everyone was afraid of him and kept their kids away from him. After all, he had bitten someone who was around him all the time. My husband and I thought we could keep the kids and the dog separated. "Don't touch the doggy!" became part of the household conversations. Now, kids will be kids and dogs want to be around people. The kids loved their dog and, Klansey being an indoor dog, it was impossible to keep them separated. I kept hearing from others, "What if it happens again? It could be worse! How would you feel if one of them lost an eye? Your kids come first!"

After crying off and on for more than a week, I decided to look for a home for Klansey. I was hoping for an older couple with no kids or a single adult. I felt that I could be picky and find the right home. There was no other choice. I also passed the word at the different animal shelters. When I contacted the shelter in Buena Vista, the staff person recommended Judy Moore as a successful dog trainer. I gave Judy a call, and Klansey and I started our dog obedience training the next week. After the first week, both the dog and I were happier. I could sense a difference even in such a short period of time. We continued practicing for several weeks.

Judy helped me to see that it is not just dog training but also people training which is needed. Our family now seems to be more aware and respectful of Klansey. Klansey knows what is expected of him and behaves accordingly. He wants to please us, and now he knows how. He will remain in our family. I think back every now and then about how I almost gave away our buddy and companion. I am so glad I searched for help.

If a dog does not feel threatened, he does not need to be defensive. When a dog learns that he can ask his owner for answers, the weight of the world is lifted off his shoulders. He can live confidently for the first time, not always looking over his shoulder and wondering what next is going to happen to him. I have found that when a dog can have peace of mind and live with confidence, he finds it much easier to be social without specific socialization training. Listen to another owner tell of coming out of the darkness of frustration into the light of peace with her dog:

We got Breeze when she was 8 months old. She has papers and is a pure black German Shepherd although we question her bloodline. At the time we got Breeze, my husband was working out of town and we were preparing to move. We lived in a small trailer for 6 weeks, waiting for our house, so Breeze was never settled and really high strung. She spent lots of time in the car or pet porter.

When we moved to our house, we hoped the yard and stable home would calm her down. Instead, she

proved difficult to potty train, going all over the house and garage even if we were home with her. For this reason we hoped she could stay in the fenced yard while we were gone. She jumped the fence and attacked the neighbor's dog several times, despite punishment. We put her on a chain and she broke it.

We put up electric fence and she barked at it constantly for hours 'til our neighbors called the police. She ended up on a three-foot chain in the garage unless we were right with her.

I couldn't walk her, she was too strong and out of control. We got her spayed, hoping it would help, but it really didn't. We do have another dog, a real mild-mannered sweetheart, so she always had company, although she's bullied him all their lives. Breeze has always been afraid of humans. She wouldn't let anyone touch her, even at our home. She never liked to be cuddled or loved—a couple minutes and she had to break away. She snapped out of fear and bit me twice, not breaking skin, but bruising.

When we started hiking in the back country, I wanted to take the dogs. Breeze wanted to go, but was stressed the entire time. I was afraid we'd meet another dog and she'd attack, so I decided to see if training would help at age 4 years. We both think Judy's ideas are great and have made a huge difference.

Breeze and I worked hard on the training for 4

months, every day, until time crunch and slow progress made me so stressed I stopped the daily routine and started to just try for some good exercise, which all three of us needed. Once I reduced my stress level, Breeze reduced her stress level too.

Breeze did well when we followed the "ritual" the same every time. She also made great progress as we were able to attend weekly group sessions and face other dogs.

Breeze has progressed so well that she has met other dogs while hiking and being off leash and has been bossy, but not vicious. I can allow the dogs to be loose in our yard or out at a job site and know Breeze will come when called. Now we can travel and spend more time together, because she is learning to control her urges and impulses. I can walk both dogs at once and even ride a bike with both dogs on leash without much difficulty. Who would ever have believed it a year ago?!

The characteristics of confidence and self-esteem are essential to all beings, not just *human* beings. *Dogs need confidence and self-esteem just as we humans do.* In saying that, I'm not anthropomorphizing dogs. Too many people adopt anthropomorphic attitudes toward their dogs. If we anthropomorphize dogs, then we agree they need confidence only because that is a quality humans need. We must go deeper than that and understand that dogs need confidence as dogs, not because we want to think of them as human-like.

Perhaps you know the philosophical statement, "You can tell the size of a man by what it takes to get his goat." If a man knows who he is and trusts where he stands in life in relation to others, he lives his life with openness and generosity and is slow to react negatively to or judge others. Similarly, when a dog feels good about himself and has confidence in his place, purpose and value, he is able to accept others around him, humans and dogs alike, much more readily. Dogs without a good sense of themselves develop a defensive attitude and show more aggression. When a seemingly aggressive dog develops greater self-esteem through dialogue with his human partner, the beautiful, good dog that has always been there shines through!

When Yogi was 16 months old, we were overjoyed to have made such a fantastic purchase. He was and still is a very handsome example of the German Shepherd dog. We thought that after owning several dogs over the years, finally we were to be proud owners of "The Perfect Dog!" At 16 months Yogi was still immature physically and mentally.

He wasn't too sure about the world around him and new situations. My friends' immediate response to Yogi was paradoxical. At first they were impressed by his magnificent appearance (about 100 pounds), but then questioned his shyness and his desire to run and hide from them. "What kind of behavior is that for a German Shepherd?" "How weird!" they would say. Of course my heart sank—our "Perfect Dog" was not supposed to be like this!

Within 6 months time Yogi became more mature, and this is when real trouble began. Now he was displaying a strong, protective character whenever anyone came to visit. We realized German Shepherds are protective by nature, but this was too much. So many times we had been embarrassed by his unfriendly and threatening behavior and just hated the unkind comments of family and friends. We just felt we didn't need this. Yogi was *not* the "Perfect Dog!" What were we to do with this beautiful social misfit?

Fortunately, we met with Judy Moore and were completely encouraged by her understanding of Yogi. We were relieved to have someone who appreciated Yogi for *himself*. Basically, we all agreed Yogi was sweet, fun-loving and sensitive. We worked on stretching those good qualities into the areas which put Yogi on the defensive.

New people and new situations were stressful for Yogi, so we set to work on getting him to focus on his handler. This was extremely important because it relieved him of having to deal with everything and everyone in his environment at one time, thus reducing his level of anxiety.

Gradually his level of trust and self-confidence increased. This was further enhanced during class time when all the dogs were put on the down-stay command. During this exercise, strangers walked slowly around and between the dogs in a non-threatening manner.

Through consistently working with Yogi in and out of class and by being keen observers of people and situations, we are able to control Yogi's behavior not only to the satisfaction of others but to Yogi's well-being as well.

These owners had sought ongoing help from a dog trainer in the state in which they previously lived, all to no avail. We are all very glad they relocated across the country to my neighborhood. I regularly dogsit for former students. The dogs share the same yard and house-space with each other and my own dogs. Sometimes a visitor to my ranch will comment on how harmoniously several dogs may be playing or snoozing together in my yard. The visitor is always surprised and impressed when I inform him that the dogs all come from different homes. Yogi's first time to stay with me was only a few weeks after he and his owner completed my training program. This big, beautiful dog, which had previously been far from perfect with other dogs, shared that yard peacefully and happily with all the other dogs for three weeks.

Emotional IQ

There is a lot of talk these days about the need for taking something dubbed "emotional IQ" into consideration when evaluating the intelligence (the standard IQ thing) of humans. I am no expert on the field of emotional IQ, but I have observed attitudes in dogs that might as well be attributed to a doggy emotional IQ. It is so important that we consider this issue of attitudes carefully.

Too often I hear someone assess their dog's potential for training with statements like "He's very smart," or "He's stubborn," or "I had another dog that was really smart, but this one seems to be pretty dense. I wonder if anything can be done with him." I can't help giving a knee-jerk response of "All dogs are smart." I no more like to hear a dog accused of being stupid than I like to hear a person, child or adult, being labeled stupid. Such judgments cannot be fairly made until we understand what makes the person or the dog tick.

What makes the dog tick is primarily the instinctive language that is bred into him, his inborn rule book. Different breeds of dogs may be prompted by their specific instincts to respond differently to the same situation. We may be tempted to judge what we perceive to be a dog's intelligence based on the responses his instincts dictate. It appears to be a dog's instinctive language that determines his emotional IQ. I will not attempt to discuss all the differences in emotional IQ among breeds. A few generalizations about breed types can be enlightening, however.

Husky breeds have been given a very bad rap, even by their breeders. I will never agree with those who say these breeds cannot be obedience trained, that they are stubborn and/or stupid. Huskies take to my training method very well indeed. The owner of a Husky or Husky mix needs to understand that more effort is going to be needed on the owner's part. However, no different nor more difficult method is needed. Huskies respond to the same procedures that I use for all other breeds. But a Husky may require more relentless persistence in patient, precise, and loving repetition of the exercises for a longer time than a dog of some other breed.

If I were to give Husky behavior a label, that label would read "Doggy Attention Deficit Disorder." That is a label that may give you an idea of the *appearance* of Husky behavior. It is not a true clinical diagnosis. They are not deficient animals and they have no actual deficits. But they do have an influential ancestral background. Huskies have been used through the ages as third-world transportation machines. Throughout their history, brute strength and toughness mattered far more than a disposition responsive to humans. Little encouragement was given to qualities such as attentiveness, gentleness, and sensitivity. There was nothing wrong with these qualities if they appeared, but they were not a desirable trade-off for power and stamina and resilience—an ability to withstand harsh, uncomfortable conditions and keep on keeping on without expecting someone else to intervene and make things easier.

In developing dialogue with a Husky, we are asking him to tune in to humans, seek and come to actually *desire* their help and accept their guidance. This relationship with a caring human is all so foreign, evolutionarily speaking. It takes time. A lot of "overriding" of inborn information must take place. For quite awhile it will appear that though the spirit of the dog is willing, the body just gets up

Huskies also dialogue

and walks away for no apparent reason. But patient repetition of corrections with no ill temper by the owner will result in the needed behavior modification.

I already referred to the impulsive behavior exhibited by the shepherding breeds. However, shepherding dogs rate highly with most people when it comes to measures of "intelligence" because of their emotional IQ. They have been bred for centuries to work fist in glove with man in the agricultural business of tending herds. They only need to sharpen their natural inclination to tune in to humans. But they need patient repetition of exercises to enable them to override their impulse to herd anything that moves.

Recently I heard a " to give away" ad aired on the radio. A six-month-old Border Collie was being advertised as needing to go to a "working" (that is, sheep-ranching) home as he was much too instinct-driven to make a family pet. Such an unfair judgment!

Border Collies can make wonderful family pets if they are given the dialogue they need and deserve.

Some of the hunting breeds such as Retrievers have evolved working closely with man and find attentiveness comes easily. Other hunting breeds which have a role of searching out game independently of man find it less natural to relate closely to humans. They are not stubborn or dull, just less responsive because of a personal agenda dictated by their particular emotional IQ. It can take awhile for a Setter to be able to hold an unmoving **sit-stay** when he sees a bird fly low over his head. But he can learn to do it through patient repetition of the exercise. Then his life will no longer be in danger when a bird or rabbit moves in the direction of a busy highway. Dialogue with his human partner will override his inborn imperative to follow in hot pursuit.

Terriers are basically hunting breeds, and in addition to having high metabolisms, they listen to strong inner dictates. But the dialogue of WR-DOS has never failed with these breeds either. Let me again emphasize, as I have before, that the owner's patience, persistence, and clear conviction of the vital life-saving importance of training are all that are needed. The system works if the owner works it.

Any breed can be a joy to share life with. I have scarcely begun to touch on the variety of breed characteristics. Many more could be explored. So many breeds have been maligned because they are not understood, particularly German Shepherds, Rottweilers, Doberman Pinchers, Pit Bulls, and Sharpeis. Even the more innocuous-looking Australian Shepherds, Dingos and Heelers have run amuck of humans all because of the instinctive language which dictates their behavior. But the emotional IQ of all these breeds fosters an enthusiastic response to human guidance when we give them a way to override their instincts and escape from impulsive behavior.

If dogs are ever to gain self-esteem, we must think of them as distinct identities deserving to be treated with consideration and respect.

Ensuring Successful Dialogue

Conversation the key ingredient

As we have seen, training should really be an unending dialogue between the dog and his human partner. This dialogue is comprised of conversational elements in addition to the main components, the exercises. Stop for a moment and consider natural canine behavior. Wild canines communicate with each other by body positions and gestures, yes, but also with voice. Coyotes and wolves yip and howl to celebrate; they yap and howl to warn; they whine and howl to mourn. Canines both wild and domestic are highly vocal.

Pleasant human chatter directed toward the dog is delightfully sufficient to send many dogs into ecstasy. Any words, any language, will do for the palaver. It is voice *tone*, not content, that counts. Using a high energy voice like Minnie Mouse works wonders, especially with a noticeably frightened dog. Dogs appear to be starved for conversation and are literally mesmerized by an enthusiastic, exciting conversationalist.

Because of this natural canine tendency to be vocal, a handler simply *must* learn to use virtually constant vocal conversation with his dog throughout his practice with the dog. Even if the handler is not naturally talkative himself, he must become so with his dog because without the conversation, training efforts will yield poor results. All the training procedures I will be explaining use constant conversation with the dog to lead the dog into the correct responses.

In order to understand how you will verbally lead your dog into correct responses, think back to a game you very likely played as a child. If you ever played the party game "Hotter-hotter, Colder-colder," you have experienced being verbally led. In that game, you stand blindfolded in a strange room with an unknown destination as the game's goal. You are entirely dependent on your party friends guiding your steps with a continual chant of, "You're getting warmer, you're getting warmer, you're HOT!" Or, "You're colder, FREEZING, now warmer, warmer"....etc.

Let's say your friends all choose to remain absolutely silent once you are blindfolded. If you are a very small child, chances are pretty good that within a few moments you will lose all your confidence in this game and begin to cry! So it is with your dog. When you begin teaching him exercises, he might as well be "blindfolded in a strange room." He does not know what the command words mean, and he has no hope of guessing.

This is what you do to lead the dog into the correct responses. First, you give the command word in a tone specific to that command (more about that in later chapters). Then you make the dog's body assume the required position while at the same time giving the dog all the credit with an extremely enthusiastic approving voice tone. Your conversation following the command word, using whatever words are convenient, provides a radar beam of sound on which your dog can home in. This conversation I call "praise-in-anticipation," and it is entirely *vocal* (accompanied by your beaming countenance). I use "that-a-way" and "that's right" most of the time because I can say them easily without biting my tongue. You *must not pet* your dog during praise-in-anticipation.

Why do I call this verbal approval praise-in-anticipation? The expression reminds you of an important attitude. The term indicates that you choose to believe that your dog, if he knew what you wanted, would do it precisely. You shower praise on him while he is assuming the correct position (entirely with your help in the beginning – remember the Swahili/glass analogy). No dog should have to wait until he has completed some exercise to get his first encouraging word. Praise comes for every move in the correct direction (i.e. "You're getting warmer!").

Whenever your dog's enthusiasm and/or confidence lags, use a revved up voice tone to encourage him. The bottom line in this training is that you create the situation which causes the dog to do that for which your command asks (you "put him there"), and you give the dog all the credit (constant praise-in-anticipation). It is such a positive experience for the dog that within minutes he is feeling as if he is on top of the world. He may have little idea of what he has done to deserve such effusive praise, but repetition in practice will in a short time show him a connection between the command word and his body's response (which you continue to bring about as long as is necessary).

The approving conversation lifts the spirits of a timid dog, literally selling him on the idea that he can be confident and trusting. Timid or not, a dog will be very attentive to "reading" your language (voice, body, energy) and responding to you because he wants to do whatever it takes to keep himself within that approving conversation. You are the constant of love, expressed as appreciation and approval, in the dog's life.

So how do you say to a dog, "You're getting colder"? You give the "correcting tone." I say *the* correcting tone because there is one specific tone which works for all dogs, even if they have never been given any language in common with humans. That tone I spell "eh" (think short "e" vowel sound as in "get"), and it is made once, forcibly in staccato fashion, from the diaphragm. I was told decades ago somewhere that it simulates a mother dog's vocal tone of correction as she snaps at her puppies. The correcting tone is not scolding. It is an "oops" message, that "gong sound" that says, "You made a mistake." That is *all* it says. It does not say the dog is bad. Nor is it followed by a tirade of verbal abuse telling the dog how rotten he is. Rather, because the correcting tone will cause the dog to momentarily cease whatever wrong he is committing, it is followed by lots of that "praise-in-anticipation" which guides, even persuades, the dog into appropriate behavior. And thereby his confidence is maintained and nurtured because he knows what he *is* to do, not just what he is *not* to do.

One student told me of a most interesting experience with this universal correcting tone. She was jogging one morning with her dog alongside her, and another large dog, strange to her, began coming toward her and her dog rather intently, giving no sign of a jolly greeting. She said she looked at the strange dog and issued the loudest, sharpest "eh" she could, and the dog stopped dead in its tracks and approached no closer. She was amazed and grateful that this appeared to be effective with any dog, trained or not. I have used it successfully many times myself as well with untrained dogs. I will not demonstrate the correcting tone for a student when a dog is with us because the dog, upon hearing it, will always be offended and misunderstand. The correcting tone should be reserved for stopping wrong behavior and never used otherwise.

Another rule governing the dialogue: never repeat command words. Why? Simply because it does no earthly good to repeat something that the dog does not understand anyway. (Remember the Swahili-speaking gentleman yelling *"HAND ME THAT GLASS!!!!"*?). This point is so important, I will drive it home with another illustration. Let's say you have a math tutor who hands you a sheet of paper with a complex math problem written across the top. You fill the page with calculations, and at the bottom you put the answer you have come up with. Your tutor walks by, looks at the page, and tells you your answer is incorrect due to a mistake somewhere in all those calculations. He then hands you another identical sheet of paper with the same problem written across the top and tells you to do the problem again. At that you are rightfully distraught. If you had known where in the page of calculations you were making a mistake, you would not have made it the first time! You do not need a simple repetition of the problem.

Similarly, do not repeat the problem for your dog. The dog which makes a mistake does not need to have the command repeated. He needs to have the mistake pointed out (the correcting tone) and corrected very immediately and precisely, which you do by physically putting him into the proper position, praising him all the while with praise-in-anticipation. Never wait for the dog to try to guess what he did wrong and how he can correct himself. That creates instant anxiety and unhappiness, a great loss of confidence on the part of the dog, and *no learning takes place*!

Earlier in this chapter I discussed the importance of praise-in-anticipation for leading the dog into correct behavior. There is another form of praise that is also vitally important to the learning process. I call it "praise-in-response." It is the final, absolutely uninhibited showering of words *and petting* on the dog which rewards his completed exercise. Praise-in-response also breaks that exercise so that the dog is at that point ready for a new activity. (As you may have guessed, this praise is the equivalent for the dog of the money the Swahili-speaking gentleman gave you.)

Consistency is paramount in your communication with your dog if you are to be kind and fair to him. When your dog does something correctly, your response must be 100% approving *every time*. When your dog does something incorrectly, your response must be the correcting tone *every time*. Think of your approving responses as white paint and your correcting responses as black paint. You only have those two paints. There can be no mixing, no gray paint. Everything the dog does is either entirely correct, and you paint him up royally with white, or it is entirely wrong, and for that moment you use only black paint. At any given moment the dog is either all right (white) or all wrong (black). To approve a partially correct action is to use gray paint. Gray paint means you and the dog are negotiating (or are perhaps confused) as to what is really correct. Remember, behavior problems are the outgrowth of a dog's uncertainty and confusion. Similarly, to refuse to properly praise a correct action by the dog at one moment because his behavior the moment before was not praiseworthy is also to use gray paint.

It is also using gray paint to let your moods influence your response to your dog's behavior. If yesterday was a great day and something the dog did (perhaps a rowdy greeting) was just fine with you, it must also be just fine with you for him to behave that way today as well, even if you are overwhelmed with distressing challenges in your life. Likewise, if you had a bad day yesterday, and something the dog did was unacceptable to you then, it must remain unacceptable today even if this is the happiest day of your life. A dog cannot understand your mood swings, and it is unjust for you to respond to his behavior as if he could. Obviously, this training stuff is character-building for humans! In WR-DOS, the language used in dialogue is very specific. No overtones!

Accessing WR-DOS

Once you have installed WR-DOS in your dog, you, his handler, must make a determined effort to follow exactly the necessary procedures for executing the exercises when you practice with your dog. To execute an exercise, you give the command word (and hand signal if required) and accompanying body movement to physically assist the dog to respond to you with the correct movement. If you like the computer analogy, you can think of practice of an exercise as "accessing" an exercise that was installed in the dog.

You learned very specific procedures to use in the installation process. With some exercises, repetition or practice of the exercise involves all the same procedures that were used to install the exercise initially. With some exercises, however, only some of the procedures required for the installation are needed when the exercise is repeated in practice (specifics for each exercise are covered in later chapters). In any case, once the dog has learned the command words through association and responds with a reflex action, the procedures which were used originally for installation are no longer necessary. The command word and hand signal alone bring the correct response.

You can see that practicing the exercises (accessing WR-DOS) means you are carrying on the dialogue with the dog via the exercises he has learned. When you practice, you must adhere strictly and consistently to the rules of this conversation (rules fully explained in the next section). To be able to adhere strictly to these rules, people need some very specific retraining. Though the language itself is quite simple, the concept of dialogue is a new and challenging way for most people to think about their interactions with their dogs. My primary and most demanding task is to teach people a new understanding of dogs and dog behavior, so that they can retrain themselves to eliminate their *own* counterproductive reflex responses to dogs.

One of the most common human reflex responses is to physically control a dog's behavior, as with a leash or some other device. Your society has programmed you to think you should control your dog with a leash at all times (ever notice all the signs at trails and parks showing a dog pressing forward against a leash?). Leashes are *not* to be used to control the dog. While the dog is learning new behavior, the leash provides assurance that he will not get himself into an unsafe situation. Also, you will use the leash to assist a dog in correctly executing an obedience exercise. But physical control is out of place in communication with your dog at any time other than when physically assisting him to do an exercise. And then such control must follow the specific guidelines for the exercise. To attempt to physically control a dog is to abandoned the dialogue.

A second universal human reflex is to punish a dog when he makes a mistake. Punishment is a very counterproductive response to any dog behavior. Punishment dissolves the glue that bonds man to dog. This glue is the mutual exchange of unconditional love. In the dialogue, the dog must know that his human partner is the constant of love for him. Because the dog is aware of that constant love, there is no reason for him to develop resistance and avoidance behavior or other defensive tendencies.

There will be some situations in which the dog needs an answer about what to do, but none of the exercises provides the appropriate response from his human partner. Yet you still need to stay within the rules of WR-DOS. For example, if the dog is making a mistake (like getting into the garbage), you need to use a creative alternative to scolding or punishment in order to maintain the dialogue. The correcting tone discussed earlier is the simple way to notify the dog of mistakes of all kinds.

When any mistake in behavior is made, use this procedure: sound the sharp correcting tone with appropriate volume. The dog will momentarily recoil from what he is doing (from investigating the garbage for example) and give you his attention, if only for a split second. That is when it will be important for you to have developed split-second reaction time through practice. While you have his momentary attention, you must begin that vocal praise-in-anticipation which "talks" the dog back into a behavior pattern that is acceptable. If he is getting into the garbage, you will draw him away from the garbage with your inviting voice, urging him to wander elsewhere and praising him when he does so.

The procedure just described is based on the assumption that the dog, when getting into the garbage, is not making a mistake which breaks a formal command such as "stay." If he is breaking such a command, then of course you must physically put the dog back into the correct place representing the correct behavior, giving praise-in-anticipation all the while.

Most dogs never get the positive experience of the "warmer-warmer" praise-in-anticipation. An owner is quick to yell "No!" at his dog for a myriad of reasons. However, when the dog stops the wrong behavior, what is his reward? Silence! The dog needs the immediate praise of his right action to maintain his confidence and his trust in the dialogue. He cannot trust the dialogue if he only hears what *not* to do, what is wrong to do. The approval makes clear to him what is *right* to do.

This same procedure—of using the correcting tone and praise-in-anticipation—works very effectively to teach a dog that it is wrong to playfully bite. It doesn't matter if you must repeat the correcting tone/praise treatment for play biting many, many times. It works, and with no bad side effects like causing the dog to lose his self-esteem.

The appropriate volume for the correcting tone is determined by the seriousness of the mistake the dog is making as well as his distance from you. I hope it is obvious that sniffing the pant leg of your dress pants with his wet nose is a far smaller offense and deserves a more gentle correcting tone than grabbing a beef roast off the dining room table. Volume, the punch from the diaphragm, adds harshness to the tone. The volume also has to be adjusted according to the personality of the dog. The sound of the correcting tone is amplified in the minds of super-sensitive dogs, or frightened and insecure dogs.

I mentioned at the beginning of this discussion the importance of following the necessary procedures every time you practice an exercise with your dog. The procedures require complete consistency in language (voice, body, energy). Remember, dogs learn the dialogue of WR-DOS so quickly because its language is simple, clear, and utterly consistent. Handler behavior inconsistent with the patterns the dog has learned often causes the dog bewilderment, confusion, and a loss of confidence. Consequently, the dog cannot respond to his handler correctly, nor can he feel good about himself. Not only must you, the handler, make the effort to be precise and consistent, but all other people who live with the dog should, over time, learn the same exact method of communicating with your dog.

If you were learning English as a second language, and your teacher was a Kansan, you would hear words and phrases in a particular accent. Do you think you would easily catch those same phrases if they were later fired at you by a Brooklynite or a Texan? Chances are, you would think you had failed entirely at learning English, and you might be tempted to give up the effort to communicate. But if the Kansan were to run the words and phrases by you again, you would recognize them and have renewed faith in yourself and your abilities. Over time, with lots of practice of your new English language, you would become more adept at understanding conversations modified by many accents. In the beginning of your study, however, you would learn more easily if those speaking to you kept everything as close as possible to the accent of the original words and phrases you began with. I do not think more elaboration is necessary for you to see how important it is to strive for exact precision with the dog in the early stages of his training practice.

Practice with precision

No one can learn a language without practicing that language. I would not pursue any training method that purports to require no practice. You and your dog need practice if you are going to dialogue successfully. You must commit to practicing the obedience exercises, the main components of the dialogue, with your dog every day for 10 to 15 minutes. Realize that after the first few minutes of "installing" each exercise, your dog has nothing new to learn. Now all he needs is lots of practice. Daily practice is for the dog just comfortable repetition with constant praise.

There is really no "average" for how long you will need to continue daily practice because it so much depends on the dog's breeding and his past experience. However, give yourself a goal of six months. Practice daily for six months, and chances are very good that you will never need to practice again for the remainder of your dog's life. Not a bad investment of time! If you quit too soon, you've wasted your effort. Once you recognize the value for the dog and yourself of the relationship the dialogue fosters, you will be happy to give your dog ten minutes of your day. If practice is carried out correctly, nothing else in life that I know of should make him feel more pleased with himself.

When your dog instantaneously responds to the command words alone, you may consider your training complete. Be sure, however, that if a rabbit runs past, your dog will still look to you for direction and respond to the command word you reply with! Of course, your dog may beg you to continue the practice routine indefinitely as it has very likely become his favorite "game," more important and certainly as enjoyable as play.

Here are some suggestions for making your practice most beneficial. For the initial practice sessions, choose a location as devoid of distractions as possible. This helps both you and the dog to focus on the work at hand. Whether you or the dog has the most difficulty focusing will depend on your individual natures, but it is not uncommon for the owner to have the greater difficulty! If you do not have a distraction-free location, convince yourself that you can practice successfully anyway.

When no options were available, I have trained dogs in many challenging environments. I have used the exercise yard of an animal shelter, with dogs staked out around my practice space. I have taught dogs and people in public parks with busy city streets as boundaries, children playing, and dogs running to and fro. Much to my surprise and delight, I have found the practice works in these situations, too. I just have to work harder to hold the dog's attention.

Dogs love to practice their WR-DOS! Just because both you

and the dog are having such a good time, do not get carried away and drill for 45 minutes. Limit practice sessions to 10 to 15 minutes each, with only 5 to 10 minutes for puppies under three months. It is certainly fine to practice as often as three or four times in a day, if you have the time. Your dog will love it, and his learning curve will soar.

In your practice sessions, take the exercises one at a time until you become proficient with each exercise. Work on the first exercise daily until you feel both you and your dog are doing it correctly. Then add the next exercise to your daily practice and become proficient with that one. Keep adding the exercises, one at a time, until you are practicing all of them with the dog every day. When the dog knows an exercise well enough that his confidence is not easily shaken, deliberately raise the level of distractions. Even hire distractions (children on bicycles, for example) if needed.

The exercises can, as I have explained before, function as therapy to change problem behavior that may have become habitual for your dog. For instance, a dog which is very timid and afraid to let people approach and pet him, will find it easy enough to hold a sitting position beside you when practicing the **Heel** exercise. When he has become very comfortable and happy sitting beside you this way, introduce the "threat" of people approaching him. Praise him profusely (verbally only) while he holds his position, literally giving him a sales job about his ability to hold that position and your faith that he is capable of doing so. Remember, he will be loathe to do anything to interrupt that immensely supportive conversation coming from you. If he moves, simply give a correcting tone and reposition him as you have learned to do for that exercise, and resume the praise. Each time he manages to hold the position just a little more confidently for just a little longer, you have given him some very positive therapy.

Using the exercises in this way is how I rehabilitate dogs. There are many, many behavior problems which crop up with dogs as a result of their personalities and experiences, and there are several exercises. So the therapeutic combinations are far too many to discuss here. As you become familiar with the exercises and give your dog's behavior some thought, you will develop creative ways, using the exercises, to help him change his behavior for the better.

Just remember, in all cases your goal is for your dog to be able to respond in a crisis, when his mind is blown. Ultimately, with every dog you will want to practice the exercises in the midst of chaos.

At the end of a practice session, allow the dog to be quiet and passive for a half hour or so. Every dog should have a place to call his own where he knows there is an invisible, yet understood, "Do Not Disturb" sign posted. It may be as formal as a crate or as informal as a pillow or rug in the corner of a room. A dog is not a toy, on call for entertainment 24 hours a day. He will learn that when he is in his "quiet spot," everyone leaves him alone. When he is ready for attention or play, he will present himself in some other location. Some dogs want very little alone time; but it should be his option. After his practice time, he may or may not choose to be in his quiet spot for his quiet time, but leave him alone anyway. Just be sure he knows you are very pleased with him. After this quiet time, by all means feel free to give him play time!

At this point you may be asking, will it require weeks or months before I see any change in my dog's behavior? In my work with dogs, I expect to see major changes in behavior in the form of attentiveness and calmness in two to five minutes! The exciting thing is, when *you* learn WR-DOS sufficiently, *your* dog will respond that quickly, too. How fast he responds will be a measure of how thoroughly you've learned the language of the dialogue.

Over time you will "flesh out" the core framework of obedience exercises which you practice with your dog. Gradually you will add many other less specific words and phrases to the six formal command words in your dog's vocabulary so that all needs in your life with your dog are covered by adequate communication.

Points to Ponder

Think about these three statements, and apply these ideas to your training practice techniques:

1. You increase a dog's capacity for attentiveness by holding him responsible for accuracy in all his exercises.

2. A dog is a thinking animal which learns by reasoning from the situations you provide.

3. An indefinite and inconsistent approach to dog handling constitutes a major cruelty. The cruelest correction is the ineffective correction because it does nothing but confuse the dog, increase his insecurity, and encourage him to further resistance. In correcting, you must be loving, consistent, and relentless. A student once described me as a cross between St. Francis of Assisi and Attila the Hun. A pretty good assessment of the attitude required for training.

Laugh as you learn

Just as a willingness on your part to be precise in your practice is key, so is a well-developed sense of humor! This is only one of many ways in which "dog training" can be character-building for people. There are many times when a sense of humor helps immensely. And of course, anger is totally unacceptable in communicating with a dog. A sincere, healthy sense of humor is an asset you must have as you begin to understand that your dog takes 90 to 95 percent of your mental focus, leaving you only five to ten percent for remembering, among other things, which is your right foot and which your left! When you are properly focusing on the dog's behavior, it may be challenging to remember your own name. So you will initially be trying to follow instructions and learn what seems like a gazillion picky details of precision with only five to ten percent of your mental capacity. Without a strong sense of humor about yourself, you could get conned into believing yourself to be an idiot, with your dog appearing to be an Einstein.

The solution to this dilemma of limited mental capacity is to begin each exercise with private practice time by yourself when you can focus 100 percent on the procedures required of you in executing the exercises. Do this where your dog cannot see or hear you—not so that he won't be laughing, but so that he won't wonder if he should be responding. As you get the picky instructions sorted out, and they become somewhat habitual, you can relegate them to just five or ten percent of your mental capacity. At that time you can begin practicing with your dog. The dog will not have had to suffer through your bloopers, and you will feel much greater self-esteem.

When I am working with a dog, I am so unaware of my surroundings or others within my surroundings that the possibilities for embarrassment are great. Someday I shall get a shirt, to wear as a uniform, which declares "WATCH OUT! I'M OPERATING ON 10%!" It is a good idea when practicing with your dog to consciously give yourself permission to be oblivious to what is going on around you. After all, it is only for ten minutes at a time.

A new leash on life

So, you have a new puppy, or you have had a dog for some time. When is it right to give the dog this new lease on life? Right now! As soon as the puppy can walk is not too soon, and that means at weaning time for most breeds. And it is never too late. I trained a 13-year-old German Shorthaired Pointer. She responded enthusiastically in the same time-frame as all others, and the remainder of her life was happier and safer for herself and her owners. Consider this example if you have had a dog for several years and question whether the training is worthwhile or effective for a dog of advanced years.

8 weeks old and HEEL is a snap

You may question the need for training your dog if your dog has never caused you any great problems. But realize that this training I am talking about is first of all *for the dog's benefit.* As I see it, untrained is unloved. Because your dog has been a delight to you, all the more does he deserve the blessing and the fun of dialogue with the human he loves. Give him this gift, and *you* will benefit in ways you cannot now even guess. Lastly, if you need a bottom line, here is one: in our litigious society, being certain that your dog does not someday inadvertently cause someone else a problem makes *economic* sense to you.

PHOTO MOMENTS

COME-ing through without distraction

Practice of COME with two at once is twice the fun

SECTION II

MAKING IT HAPPEN

PHOTO MOMENTS

These dogs would love to play, but only if invited

**These dogs are in dialogue with their owners
(despite distance), and I can't distract them**

CHAPTER 5

Attention Please!

Chapters five through ten will take you step by step through the *how* and *why* of installing WR-DOS in your dog. The obedience exercises of **Sit, Sit-Stay, Heel, Down, Down-Stay, Stand, Stand-Stay,** and **Come** are the main components of the dialogue you and your dog will enter into and maintain for your lifetime together.

My training method demands that you follow the instructions to the letter and be absolutely consistent and precise in doing the exercises with your dog. Please recognize that my method is not fussy, it is effective. If a dog can be doing all the exercises in only 15 minutes—which I see happen for me with virtually every dog—then the precision is worth it. And realize that the more precise and consistent you are, the easier and more pleasant the activity is for both you and your dog. Remember, practice of the exercises should be as enjoyable for the dog as play.

Before you begin learning how to do the exercises precisely, you must know what equipment to use. In pursuing this training, you do not need much equipment, but it must be the right equipment:

Chain training collar

For correct size, take the dog's neck measurement and to that add four inches. Buy a collar of the heaviest links obtainable in the length you need (they tend to easily break) and avoid those which have extra rings or snaps attached. Dog trainers are waging a great debate over use of a chain collar. Because traditional training relies on controlling the dog physically with a leash and collar, the debate between

Simple equipment

trainers over use of the chain collar centers on whether the chain collar, when used for physical control, is more injurious to the dog than some other kind of collar. Their debate misses my point—that physical control is out of place and communication is all that counts. If the dog hangs on your words rather than your leash, he will not be injured by a properly fitted chain collar.

I use a chain collar for two reasons only: (1) It is the only collar the dog cannot back out of in a moment of resistance, hence a safety factor; and (2) the jingle of the chain provides just another little sound element of the language we use.

The collars are sometimes called "check chains" or "choke chains." We will not use the collar as a check chain, since we are not using the leash and collar to control (check) the dog. A dog *can* choke with a chain collar if he is left wearing one when unattended and he happens to catch it on something. One time a very distraught dog-owner called to tell me the tragic news that during her absence her very small dog had fallen over the edge of her deck. Its chain collar had caught between two deck boards, and the dog had hung. I only mention such an unpleasant incident to drive home this point: *Never* have a chain collar on your dog unless you are practicing exercises with him!

The correct way to position collar

The jingley sound of the chain collar is, among other things, a happy sound for the dog. Remember, done correctly, training practice is as much fun for the dog as play. He soon associates the sound of the chain collar with this wonderful activity with you. If I pick up a chain collar within earshot of whatever dogs are at my house, what howling and fussing ensues! Hearing the unavoidable rattle and jingle of the collar, each dog anticipates that maybe this time it will be *his* turn to practice!

Flat leather or nylon web leash

The leash should be six feet long with a trigger snap. Other snaps will work but can be bothersome. A 1/2-inch to 5/8-inch wide leash is adequate for all dogs. Do not burden yourself with handling a wide, heavy, triple-stitched monster of a leash. Remember, you are not going to control your dog with a leash. And after you have completed your training with your dog, a thread will suffice (in order to comply with leash laws)! *No flexi-leads.* I'll explain why in the discussion of the first activity of attention-getting.

You are now ready to initiate dialogue with your dog. You will recall that dialogue requires the dog to be attentive to you at all times with his eyes and his ears so that he can receive information from you about what he should be doing at any given moment. You will never command him to be attentive. It is something that simply becomes the way your dog lives his life. You will help him develop that attentiveness by means of a walking activity.

I will call this first activity with the dog an exercise because that term fits the format you are expecting for training—a series of exercises. However, with this "exercise" you will be setting up a circumstance from which your dog will learn how he must behave at all times *other* than when he is on a specific formal command—doing some formal exercise. So this first one is not so much an exercise as it is *life itself.* But I need a word, so "exercise" is it.

For this exercise you must simply become a very erratic individual—when you are walking with your dog, that is. First, understand clearly that there is no unwritten law or ethic demanding that you walk at all times only where the dog wants to walk. You have a right, when you walk any dog, to decide where you are going to go and at what pace. You will, however, only find this possible with your own dog which you have trained to be attentive, or another dog which has been similarly trained. Anytime you put your dog on a leash to walk with you, he must not set his own course and drag you after him. He must stay in dialogue with you.

Let's imagine that you are teaching your dog to live within a "bubble" with you. The leash length represents the radius of the bubble. The dog is free to do whatever he wants within the bubble, but only *you* can move the bubble from place to place. If the dog touches the end of the leash, he is leaving the bubble. (This is why the flexi-leads cannot be used. They require the dog to pull against them.) The dog must not leave the bubble because his only safety

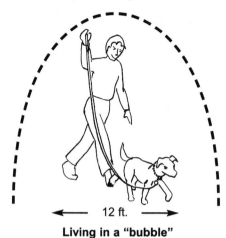

12 ft.

Living in a "bubble"

is in living in relationship to you where he can get the answers he needs.

Begin this exercise with the handle of the leash in your right hand, thereby giving the dog the entire six feet of leash. Hold your hand at least shoulder-high, high enough so that when the dog is close to you, the leash does not drag on the ground where the dog can step over it. Do not decide to let your arm be lazy and take up the extra length of leash in your left hand. The dog must have the six-foot "bubble" radius within which to move. Say the dog's name, followed by an informal command, an invitation, such as "Let's go for a walk," "Let's go" or Let's walk." This is the only informal

**Leash dangles from
raised right hand**

command you will use in the exercises you practice daily, and it is helpful to be consistent by using the same words each time. Since this command is only an invitation, you may repeat it in your conversation of praise-in-anticipation with the dog. But do not repeat his name in your conversation. He should be learning to expect a new directive whenever he hears his name.

As an erratic individual (for training purposes only) you adopt the habit of walking only a few steps in one direction with your dog before doing an abrupt about-face, or one-eighty (180°) as I refer to it. Do not allow the dog to reach the end of the leash in front of you at any time. The key to the effectiveness of the one-eighty is that it be done quickly from within the *slack* of the leash, giving the dog no warning. You definitely *must not* sound his name or a correcting tone or tug on the leash.

In the beginning, before initiation of dialogue, the dog will be obliviously following his nose until he comes to the end of the leash and discovers that you are now, and have been for a step or two, traveling in the exactly opposite direction to what you had been a moment before. The dog hits the end of the leash on his own. You *do not pull* on the dog. You are not punishing or correcting the dog for his inattentiveness. You will never need to do that. The dog will quickly learn to be attentive all on his own if you diligently follow my instructions.

Because you are traveling at a steady, brisk rate in a direction opposite to that of the dog when he comes up against the end of his leash, the dog will find himself turning about quite abruptly and heading in your direction. He may voice his surprise, but his sounds

Hug chest with right arm as you pivot

When dog hits end of leash, he is notified that you have left him

Dog quickly rejoins you

indicate that he is startled, not physically injured in any way, provided the leash was not caught under one of his legs (which is why it is important to keep your right hand high so the dog does not step over the leash). Because dogs are descended from predator animals designed to bring down large animals, they have very muscular necks, and it takes much more than a sudden stop at the end of a leash to do any damage.

The dog is no more offended by hitting the end of the leash than he would be if he stumbles while going up some steps. In the case of stumbling on the steps, he would not lose either confidence or self-esteem. Rather, he would be careful to lift his feet higher the next time he attempts those steps. So is it with this attention-getting. The dog is not offended when he hits the end of the leash. However, it takes only a few times at most of seeing you "leaving without warning" for the dog to become more attentive. Remember, the dog has a very strong instinctive desire to companion with you.

When the dog does his sudden turnabout in response to having gone as far as the leash allows in a direction opposite to that which you are taking, he sees one very important thing: *your back*. There are two reasons that seeing your back is *the* key to the incredible effectiveness of the one-eighty in teaching the dog attentiveness.

The first reason is that the dog wants to be sure that you are always there for him. It is precisely because you are so very important to him that this attention-teaching move (disappearing with a one-eighty) is so immediately effective. You can pull a dog back *to* you from distractions (that is, *the world* in all its enticing forms) for as long as life is long or until your arm or your patience gives out. It will not do any good. You are merely hassling the dog with these constant interruptions of his exploration of the universe via smell. Your pull on his neck means nothing. In the long term, constant hassling and scolding in this way *can* make some dogs feel crummy, irritated, even angry. However, if you threaten to leave the scene, *his* scene, that is another matter altogether!

When your dog sees your back, he perceives that the most important element of his life is walking out on him. It only takes a minute and a few of these one-eighties in rapid succession for the dog to figure out that he must keep his peripheral vision on you. And one ear cocked toward you certainly helps as well. Thus he learns to be attentive with his eyes and ears. This is the initiation of dialogue.

The second reason that seeing your back is so important is that when the dog turns and sees that you are leaving him, that is conclusive evidence for him that you are not the one who caused the startling and unpleasant disruption of his personal agenda. You did not punish him. You did not do anything to him. You simply wanted to go in a different direction. He quickly learns that it is his own inattentiveness to you that is causing those disruptions. Then he solves his own problem by paying attention to you.

When you do a one-eighty, for that moment drop your right arm across your chest, and always pivot to the right, or toward that arm. By turning to the right and fixing your arm to your chest, you will not use your arm to pull on the leash. Also, turning this way enables you to take the weight of the dog (who initially may hit the end of the leash with considerable momentum) across your body and not on your shoulder socket. If your dog weighs 80 or 100 pounds, you will have to alter his direction by literally throwing your weight against that leash as you pivot. Otherwise, you will turn your back on him and the appearance will be that of a game of tug-of-war when the dog reaches the end of the leash. The dog will not be startled. He may never even turn to see that you are leaving him.

Tug of war accomplishes nothing

After the dog turns, immediately resume the shoulder-high position with the right hand. When doing a one-eighty, there should be no correcting tone. You are not correcting the dog. You are only changing direction. The dog is doing nothing for which you would want to punish him. He is simply ignoring you. So you in effect ignore him. You do not use your voice to warn the dog of your turn because you are teaching him to keep his eye on you and stop ignoring you. Instead, you use praise-in-anticipation that never lets up. This praise is essential because it assures the dog that his relationship with you, one of love and approval, is still intact.

If distractions abound and the dog is attracted to all of them, you will need to learn to do one-eighties in rapid-fire succession. A distracted dog will rebound from hitting the end of the leash and be to the leash's end in the opposite direction in what will seem to you to be a split-second. To get the jump on him, this is a good rule to follow: repeat a one-eighty as soon as the dog passes by your knee and no later (that will be about two steps for you). As soon as the dog has regained his composure enough to give you attention, you can resume doing one-eighties every half dozen steps or so.

To the dog and any lookers-on, while you are walking this way, you appear to be totally oblivious to what the dog is doing and where he is going. This communicates to the dog that your turns are a normal part of the whole walking process and are to be expected at any moment. Of course, you will actually be paying a lot of attention to the dog in order to keep the leash from getting under his legs. Always use a vigorous pace for the walking. Be sure the leash is always slack, thereby giving the dog no hints as to your whereabouts unless he is being attentive with his eyes. Be aware of the dog's position relative to you so that you do not do a one-eighty and fall headlong over the dog's body. It is not possible to practice this exercise well if you allow yourself to be distracted. Owners, too, learn more attentiveness!

For this exercise, the dog is required to do nothing more than to be attentive. He can start moving with you from any position at all, even from having his head halfway down a hole he is digging. And when you come to a stop, he is free to hang out within the bubble in any way he chooses.

After initiation of dialogue, the dog will be walking with you rather attentively on a slack leash. However, you must remember that he needs a few minutes of practice time every day to develop constant attentiveness. Attentiveness is not a quality that is missing one moment, and then, because the correct button is pushed, is present in full-blown glory the next moment. Attentiveness begins to develop with the first session of one-eighties, but it needs nurturing practice to grow into a predominant behavioral quality. This means that you must not let a leisurely half-hour walk to the post office be substituted for a few minutes of specific practice of "several steps, about-face, several steps, about-face." Your walk to the post office probably will not be leisurely anyway as soon as the dog second-guesses that you are headed in a straight line for a distant destination and therefore abandons his attentiveness and begins to pursue his nose, once again hanging on his leash.

When you first use the one-eighty technique, the dog may, depending on his disposition, appear frustrated, offended, bewildered or even intimidated. After all, it is all a new game with a new set of rules and very mentally demanding. That is why your voice giving constant praise-in-anticipation (the "hotter- hotter colder-colder game") is so vital. The voice tone, with its constant approving, encouraging and even exciting tone, lets the dog know that everything will be all right in the end.

In his frustration/bewilderment your dog may try one of several tactics to get you to stop moving. After all, if he can get you to stop moving, there is no longer a possibility that you will leave him without warning. Therefore he can go back to checking out local smells with total focus. Some favorite tactics for accomplishing this are: sitting and refusing to move (maybe he is setting an example for what he wants you to do); getting between your legs and refusing to move (the more direct approach to persuading you to stop); jumping up and latching onto your left leg with a bear hug; and nipping you in the calf or derriere. The important thing here is that you do not get at all distracted from your intent to keep moving erratically on your own course at all costs, talking approvingly all the time. Once you learn to do this, you will no longer find it difficult to walk while at the same time staying precisely focused on what both you and the dog are doing.

Let me digress for just a moment and speak about the importance of protecting yourself from injury when practicing with your dog, not only because no one wants to be hurt, but because pain can distract you from precisely carrying out an exercise. Dogs come equipped with teeth and claws. Even the most well-meaning dog, especially a puppy with needle-sharp baby teeth, can inflict damage with those teeth and claws. Dogs may nip or scratch playfully or defensively. In either case, you will find the bites or scratches uncomfortable, and that discomfort may present a disruption to the exercise that is being practiced. I recommend that you wear gloves and long pants when practicing with your dog. Never react angrily to biting and scratching. Anger and punishment, as I have said before, are counterproductive. Every dog I have trained has inevitably progressed reasonably quickly out of biting and scratching behavior, and I have never resorted to punishment.

There are dogs—some examples are profiled in this book—which will begin the training with defensive behavior that includes serious snapping and biting at people or dogs. Such problem behavior will disappear as the dogs gain confidence, and it usually does not take long. I speak here from years of experience with rehabilitating problem dogs. However, it is really important that you use a cloth muzzle (see illustration) for such a dog if you think there is any possibility he may bite you or any other person or dog who is participating in his training. Use the cloth muzzle every practice session as just a standard part of the equipment, like the leash and collar. Since it is always used for a fun activity and not as a punishment, your dog will not be adversely affected by the muzzle. A cloth muzzle that fits properly is not uncomfortable for the dog, just unfamiliar. It will become familiar

Think of this kind of muzzle as "clothing"

with daily use.

In every case where I have had to use a muzzle initially with a dog, that dog has outgrown the need for it at some point. It may only take a day or two, or it may take several months. That time frame will depend on the rehabilitation needs of the dog and the skill of the handler.

So, with your body now adequately protected, you are walking enthusiastically but erratically with your dog. With most dogs I work with, I gain the dog's attention in one to two minutes. If your dog happens to be one of the few that is especially intent on pursuing his own agenda, this exercise could take a few minutes more. Also, if he is a young puppy, not yet acquainted with walking while connected to a leash, you will need to take more time. The more adept you become at this exercise by first practicing without your dog, the more quickly your dog will respond.

If this exercise with your dog requires a little more time, you may need frequent breaks. When you find yourself out of breath and approaching exhaustion, come to a standstill but keep talking between pants. The dog will enjoy the praise, and if you are practicing in a location free of distractions, he will probably give you his attention long enough for you to catch your breath.

Whenever you are stopped, the dog does not need to do any specific thing except continue to be attentive. He can sniff the ground around you within the six-foot radius of the leash, his bubble, but he must *never touch the end of the leash,* never leave the bubble. He can relieve himself, lie down and nap, whatever. The informal walk on leash exercise is just that—very informal. It is the exercise that basically teaches the dog how to live his life with you.

Your dog must learn this attentiveness *on leash* because with the leash connection you can create consequences of inattentiveness. If, while you are stopped, his attention wanders and he begins to approach the six-foot limit, *before* he touches the end of the leash you must instantly and abruptly turn on your heel and head off in the opposite direction. If the dog has already leaned into the leash, you must step quickly toward him so as to slacken the leash and *then* pivot and leave him. And little by little with such repeated experiences, even the most distracted dog will learn to remain attentive.

This learned attentiveness will carry over into his whole life with you when he is off leash. After he has learned the dialogue, you may, for example, have him outside with you, off leash, while you are gardening, and he will hang around you in the same way he originally learned to do within a six-foot bubble, but the bubble can now be 20 to 30 feet around you. What he will *not* do is get a whiff of something exciting down the block and respond to an impulse to go check it out. He will most likely in some way let you know that there is something interesting off yonder. Then you have the opportunity to go with him to check it out or else to communicate to him why it is not to be investigated at this time.

The dialogue concept is so vital to a dog being able to live a long, full and happy life. The dog must learn that he must never decide on his own to rush up to other animals, other people, other vehicles without you. If it is appropriate for this animal/person/vehicle to be greeted at close range, you and the dog will do it together, and you, as the interpreter of life, will lead the way. In this way, bad encounters of all kinds are avoided. Dog fights are avoided, humans are not offended, and the dog remains clear of dangerous moving vehicles. It is also the only foolproof way I know of to poison-proof your dog. He will not eat something harmful without your knowledge because he will be near you when he finds the enticing food.

I would like to quote a newspaper article that appeared in a small town paper. The article was addressing in part the shock and grief of losing beloved pets. Sentences like those quoted here have been written before and will be written again and again until there is more universal understanding of the communication that dogs need.

> "...The owners may often feel guilty, especially in the case of accidents, such as when their pet, one minute sitting quietly by their side, the next in full flight after a squirrel or rabbit, never hears the screech of brakes. The sound of the impact remains imprinted forever in the owner's memory."

So tragic. So unnecessary. It is not enough that we react to the dog's behavior. By the time we react, it is very likely too late.

Remember, the fundamental principle of my whole system of dialogue is that communication begins with a question from the dog. He must ask first whether he should chase the squirrel or not. Then we can always give him the right answer.

The do's and don't's for attention-getting

DO NOT:

- Start moving until you have said the dog's name and invited him to move with you.
- Pull on the leash.
- Start moving or walk when the leash is taut.
- Warn the dog of your change of direction.
- Use the dog's name in your praise and conversation.
- Scold or punish the dog

DO:

- Say the dog's name before you start moving and say something informal to invite him to go with you.
- Give verbal praise ("praise-in-anticipation") effusively, loudly and non-stop.
- Allow the dog to "live his life," that is, investigate, etc., as long as he does not forget you.
- Utilize every new distraction as a reason to disappear (pivot 180 degrees).

CHAPTER **6**

Side by Side Forever
(Heel on and off leash)

As soon as the dog is giving you his attention as you walk on leash, you can begin teaching him all the formal exercises. We will begin with **Sit** because the **Heel** exercise proceeds from the **Sit**.

Bend over so leash remains slack

Up on the collar and down on the rump

The **Sit** is very easy and so basic. As you are walking with the dog in the bubble (the "informal walk on leash"), maneuver yourself to the right-hand side of the dog. Work your way close to the dog as you walk, taking up the excess length of leash, using your left hand to gather it into your right hand from your left. Always leave enough leash between your hand and the dog's collar so that he does not feel any contact with the leash. To do this you will have to *bend over* as you walk. It should only take a few steps in a bent stature for you to have the leash fed into your right hand so that your right hand is down at the point where the leash snaps to the collar ring.

It is very important that you do continue walking those few steps and that you keep up the constant talking, the praise-in-anticipation. If you stop the talk and remain upright as you walk and shorten the leash, the dog not only begins to be "hung" from your hand, but he also doesn't hear the confidence-inducing praise. He will suffer at least some anxiety as he tries to guess what it is you want next. No need for this. If you shorten the leash correctly, with your body bent over, to the dog there appears to be no real change in the walking activity. The leash is still slack, and your praise keeps him walking confidently.

As soon as your hand is at the snap of the leash, come to a halt, saying the dog's name as you do so. Then immediately say the command **Sit** in a pleasant, not harsh, tone. A partial second *after* saying the command, lift up on the collar (from your right hand's position at the leash's snap), and with your left hand push down on the dog's rump so that his body assumes the sitting position. Then release him from the exercise with abundant praise-in-response.

Every time he hears the command word **Sit** for the first hundred or more times, the dog should find himself suddenly in the sitting position. Because you are putting him into the correct position, he will never make a mistake, so he will never encounter displeasure from you. He will do the exercise perfectly *each and every time* and get all the credit for it. His self-esteem will soar! We have eliminated trial-and-error learning as well as the unreliable element of luck. The dog's success is not dependent on chance. Instead, with practice over time, the dog will begin to associate the command word **Sit** with the body position in which he always finds himself right after he hears the word. With enough repetition he will develop a body reflex response to the command word **Sit**.

During the "training phase" (the first few months of practice when the dog is learning to associate the command words with the exercises), you are the one "making everything happen". During this period, if ever the dog does not sit, it will be *your* fault as the handler, not the dog's. Therefore you are not to think of repeating the command. At this point, the dog is not responding with understanding to the command word. If you failed to put him into the sitting position, he is not expected to sit. Therefore, always make the **Sit** happen. The dog must experience the absolute consistency of hearing the command word **Sit** and finding himself in the sitting position immediately afterward. If a review of this concept is needed, refer to the analogy of the Swahili-speaking gentleman in Chapter 1.

The dog has completed the **Sit** exercise as soon as his rump touches the ground. He is not required to hold the position unless the command **Sit** is immediately followed by the command **Stay**. This is a matter of precision, and precision is what makes WR-DOS so stress-free for the dogs. **Sit** is not a command with vague implications. The command means "assume a sitting position," period. It doesn't mean "hold that position for some undetermined amount of time."

If you are about to take another action that involves the dog, and you know the dog can tell what you are about to do, you can expect him to "chill out" and wait for you by holding his sitting position. (Perhaps you are holding up his collar preparatory to putting it on him, or you have your hand on the car door and are about to open it.) When you ask him to sit, give him a verbal thank-you but no praise-in-response. Rather, *quickly* proceed to what you are about to do (open the car door, for example). Since the dog can see that you are about to do a next thing which has a definite time frame, he can wait patiently for the praise-in-response which releases him. If he moves, it is legitimate to give the correcting tone and reposition him, always with accompanying praising words.

For the **Sit** exercise, it is not necessary that the dog sit in any specific position relative to your body. I ask that you work with the dog on your left-hand side during the early training period only so that there is a training progression for both you and the dog, easing you into the requirements of the **Heel** exercise.

The do's and don't's for teaching Sit

DO NOT:

- Repeat the command.
- Expect the dog to remain sitting for an indefinite period of time.

DO:

- Say the dog's name before giving the command Sit.
- Give "praise-in-anticipation" while putting the dog into position.
- Use "praise-in-response" to end the exercise.

With the **Heel** exercise, again the responsibility is on the handler to "make it happen." Begin by asking the dog to sit beside your left side (remember—put him there!). As you put him into the sitting position, you can say "thank you" or "that's right," but do not pat the dog or give any other praise-in-response which would release him from the exercise. He will therefore hold his sitting position for a moment or two while you get ready to say his name followed by the command **Heel**. But act quickly, as I said before. Otherwise the dog will be expecting praise-in-response that you do not want to give at this point.

To begin HEEL, have dog sit beside your left leg

Hold the leash doubled up in your right hand with your right arm hanging completely relaxed, slightly right of center of your body. There should be only enough leash paid out to form a shallow "U" between your hand and the dog's collar. Your arm must stay relaxed throughout the exercise as you are *not to use the leash* in any way to guide the dog. You will use your voice and body position only. After all, the goal is to have the dog perform this exercise *off leash* one day soon. So start from day one "thinking off-leash," thinking and acting as if you have no leash on the dog.

To give the **Heel** command, use a very inviting and "get-up-and-go" tone of voice. In other words, use a tone with energy. After giving the command, take the first step forward with your left foot, the foot which is next to the dog. That is part of the body language. The leg moving next to the dog invites him to think that he also should move. Be alert that you do not move the foot until you have fully completed giving the command "Heel." Just because *you* know what it is you are planning to do next, the dog still cannot read your mind. He will not know what you are going to do until you have said the command word. Therefore, only after you have said **Heel** should you make any move forward. With the very first step, begin the praise-in-anticipation to talk him along with you. Because of your inviting tone of voice and the movement of your left leg, the dog will be thinking that he should move. Your immediate praise-in-anticipation lets him know that he has guessed correctly, and he will confidently stride out with you. If he hesitates, rev up your voice and pat your left thigh to give further encouragement. Do not use the leash to make him move!

Step forward with your left foot

As I said, it is up to you to "make it happen" for this as for every command. To make **Heel** happen, you need to be alert, energetic and sometimes downright creative. For the **Heel** exercise, the dog is to move at your pace, precisely next to your left knee. Now how are you going to

Follow the dog's right shoulder as if he were your leading dance partner

"make this happen" for your dog without using the leash? To make it happen for him, *you* move at the *dog's* pace, precisely next to his right shoulder, profusely praising him all the while with your voice for how brilliant he is. Right away he enjoys the exercise because of the confidence and pride you instill in him with your praise. With repeated practice in this way, the dog begins to associate the command word **Heel**, with moving with you right next to your left leg. You will be amazed at how soon he will begin to do this on his own, and *you* will begin to have to follow *him* less.

Teach the dog to be attentive by making the practice interesting. Change direction frequently, either doing "about-faces" to the right or turning to the left. An about-face to the right is the easiest way to change direction with a dog in the heeling position because you pivot and the dog follows to the outside of your body. When turning to the left, you must be able to step completely in front of the dog so that you keep the dog to the inside of the turn and he does not simply get bumped out in front of you.

Turns to the left are an excellent means for teaching the dog not to fall into the habit of "forging" (pacing himself just slightly ahead of you) and/or sniffing the ground on the **Heel** exercise. Be sure again *not* to use the leash to guide the dog in these changes of direction. If the dog is forging and you are turning left, step quickly and agilely in front of him and pivot left. If the dog is sniffing the ground, turn left so that your foot sweeps under his nose,

Do one or more 360's to stop forging and restore attention

interrupting the sniffing. You must not hold the dog back with the leash to make this move easier for yourself! And never let up on the praise-in-anticipation. The praise builds the dog's confidence while he is learning from the circumstances you are creating.

If you are doing an about-face and the dog lags, rev up your praising voice tone and pat your left thigh with your left hand to hurry him along. *Do not pull on him with the leash.* The *only* exception to this is if your puppy is very young and resists moving entirely. Then, and only then, use the leash to *tug him into motion* and then use your voice to keep him going on a slack leash. *Do not drag him* on a taut leash to get him to move.

To keep the **Heel** interesting, you will want to change pace frequently as well. Go from "normal" (a relaxed but brisk walk) to "fast" (running walk or all-out run) to "slow" (hardly moving) and practice any combinations of these you can think of along with changes of direction. For instance, you might begin with normal, turn about, then immediately begin fast, drop to slow, and immediately turn about again. It is a game your dog will love.

The **Heel** exercise involves three "phases" for the dog: (1) starting up and moving forward with you; (2) moving at varying paces as you do; and (3) coming to an "automatic" sit in the **Heel** position (right next to your left leg and perfectly straight with the direction you are facing) whenever you stop. The dog remains on the **Heel** command until you break it with praise-in-response, even if your stop is a long one. Understand, regardless of whether your stop is short or long, you must give the command **Heel** in order to return to phase one (start up) again. That would not be repeating a command. However, to repeat the word **Heel** at any time *while you are moving* would be repeating a command. Therefore, do not say **Heel** while the dog is moving.

Halt within the HEEL exercise requires a SIT beside your left leg

During the early stages of training (for however long the early stages need to be), upon halting within the **Heel** exercise, you will give the command **Sit** and put the dog in the sitting position (see drawing for **Sit**). Remember, every time you stop moving forward, you are to ask the dog to sit beside you as you stop and, of course, put him there. Interestingly, this is a temporary command and the only temporary command ever used. In time the dog will form the body reflex habit of sitting instantly when you come to a halt, without need for any command. Understand that this "automatic sit" applies to the **Heel** exercise and not to the informal walk on leash.

> Let me remind you that the dog's name must precede every command you give, even if the command is temporary, as is the case with SIT when halting from the HEEL.

As soon as the dog is heeling attentively each time you practice, you can begin practice of this exercise off leash. Everything is to be practiced (and, more importantly, performed in real life) off leash eventually. When you decide to give the heel exercise a try off leash, first practice briefly on leash. Then halt as usual, but do not break the command. Quietly and without any fanfare unsnap the leash from the dog's collar. Just continue to carry the leash, now doubled up and out of the way, in your right hand. Don't let anything about your voice or your attitude indicate to the dog that anything about the routine is different. Continue practicing the heel exercise just as before. You will find that you now have only your voice and your body position to use to continue to "make it happen" for the dog. But that is all you were *ever* to use even when practicing on leash. Now you will find out if you really were indeed from the outset "thinking off-leash" so as not to use the leash to control the dog. If you have not been "thinking off-leash," you *will* start doing so now, guaranteed!

If the dog does not sufficiently focus on your voice and your body to do the **Heel** successfully off leash, come to a halt (taking hold of the dog and putting him into the proper sitting position in response to his name and the command **Sit**), and quietly snap the leash once again to his collar. No scolding in your voice! Resume practicing with nothing but praise-in-anticipation as if nothing wrong had happened. But now be sure you are practicing properly, using only voice and body position to make this exercise happen for the dog, and only having the leash there so that, if his attention wanders, you can do some one-eighties to get his attention back on you.

The do's and don't's for teaching Heel

DO NOT:

- Move before completion of the command word Heel.
- Use the leash to communicate with or control the dog.
- Repeat the command Heel while moving.
- Use the dog's name in your praise and conversation.
- Scold or punish the dog for his mistakes.
- Expect the dog to fix his own mistakes.

DO:

- Say the dog's name before the command Heel.
- Give the name and command invitingly before every start-up.
- Step forward with your left foot.
- Give "praise-in-anticipation" immediately, effusively, loudly and continually.
- Use the procedure for Sit whenever you stop.
- Practice different speeds and make frequent, and sometimes long, halts.
- Give the correcting tone if a mistake occurs and then fix the mistake.
- Use "praise-in-response" to end the exercise.

CHAPTER 7

Alert But Still, Calm, Confident
(Sit-stay)

There is much more involved in the **Sit-stay** exercise than meets the eye. I worked with one dog which took six months to "learn" to do **Sit-stay** successfully. It was not the command words or the body position that took the dog six months to learn. Trust had to be learned. The dog was emotionally unstable and basically felt very insecure. The **Sit-stay** exercise requires the owner to leave the dog, putting a distance between himself and the dog for some period of time. It is not unusual for a dog to find it at first impossible to hold his position while the owner steps away. Shelter dogs almost universally have difficulty with the **Sit-stay** because they are typically very insecure. A dog loses all sense of security when he finds himself abandoned to a cage at an animal shelter. The dog must have, or else through supportive dialogue attain, enough security and emotional stability to cope with being left alone as the handler walks away. Practice of the **Sit-stay** exercise gives the dog opportunity to build up calmness and confidence.

Any **Stay** exercise requires the dog to control his physical impulse to move about excitedly and his mental impulse to seek more secure surroundings (i.e., next to his owner's body). Daily practice of this exercise for some weeks will provide the dog with the ability to control his body and quiet his worried mental impulses. That is what "behavior modification" is all about. From this exercise the dog will also learn to trust that the owner will *always* return to him no matter how long it takes. It is the owner's responsibility to be sure this is always the case.

Begin the **Sit-stay** exercise by putting the dog into the sitting position in response to the command **Sit**. Always take time for at least a quick word of praise-in-anticipation. Even just a "thank you" to the dog for his sit will do. However, since you are going to move right on to a **Stay** command, do not give praise-in-response for his sit. (If you do, he will then feel specifically released from the command and able to move about.)

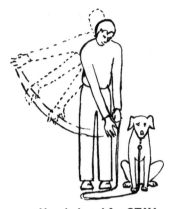

Hand signal for STAY

Now, plunge your personal energy level to zero. Check to be sure the leash is entirely "paid out" with only the handle in your *left* hand, and that it is not under the dog's or your foot, under the dog's leg, or in any way caught on or trailing over the dog's body. Then, prepare as quickly as possible to give the **Stay** command since the dog is not required to hold his sitting position unless there is some indication you are preparing to do something else with him. Extend your right arm out in front of and to the right of your right leg. Have your hand open, fingers together, palm facing the dog. Keeping your eyes on the dog's face, move this hand slowly and ever so steadily in a sweep toward the dog's face, like a stop sign, as you say the command **Stay** with a long, low, drawn-out monotone for the whole duration of the slow hand sweep. Do not let the hand come into contact with the dog, and do not hold the hand in front of the dog's face once the sweep is completed. Take the hand quietly back to your side.

Take a first step away from the dog

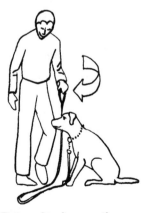

Return in slow motion

Smile with a big toothy grin

and keep your eyes on the dog's eyes. If the dog does not return your gaze, that is okay. Keep your gaze fixed and that big grin spread from ear to ear so that if and when your dog looks at you, he will see your expression. It makes it more difficult for the dog to do this exercise if you use verbal praise-in-anticipation. Your voice excites him just enough that it makes it much harder for him to understand that he is not to move. It is your voice tone and your slow, deliberate manner that communicates to the dog that he should freeze in place. But, as always, encouraging praise is very important, and this time it is conveyed only by your grinning face.

At this point, transfer the handle of the leash to your right hand. Calmly and smoothly take a first step away from the dog in a line directly in front of him, pivoting so as to keep facing him, and keep your gaze on him. Be sure to take that step with your *right foot*. For the first several times you do this exercise, try "flowing" like an amoeba. Transfer your weight and your balance onto your right foot for a step of 18 inches or so, and let your body kind of flow onto that foot so that there is no abrupt movement of your body. This body language says to the dog that he should not jump up and follow you, but continue to hold his position and see what is going to happen,. Even a dog that I have worked with for only three or four minutes (total time) can correctly read this body language.

Some dogs will immediately move from their sitting position and flow right with you as if they are attached to your legs by Velcro. No matter. If at any point after you have given the command **Stay** the dog moves at all (and this includes lying down as well as standing up or moving from his place), instantly give the dog the correcting tone and put him back into his original position.

Use the collar as much as possible to reposition him, and use your hands only when necessary. Your dog will associate an abrupt upward tug on the collar with the movements you used to initially put him into a sitting position. Too much use of hands, on the other hand, can be mistaken for a hug or petting or even play, thereby confusing the dog. Therefore that kind of correction is unfair. As you "fix the dog's mistake" by repositioning him, *do not repeat either the command Sit or Stay*. Remember, you are correcting a mistake, not presenting the exercise anew.

No matter how many times the dog moves from his position, your response is the same: a correcting tone, an unsmiling face, a repositioning of the dog, and then sunshine breaking out all over your face again. The dog is all wrong at the moment he makes the mistake, but as soon as the mistake is corrected, he is completely right once again. If you have to correct fifteen times in a row, your response is still the same. You cannot lose your patience and, having repositioned the dog, glare at him with an expression that says, "Move once more and you've had it!" Yes, dog training is character building!

No matter where you are when the dog makes his mistake of moving, you must return to the dog and reposition him. You cannot yell at him from a distance and hope that he will figure out his mistake and correct himself. This is simple injustice. The dog does not yet know what is being asked of him, and he must get the "hotter-hotter (grin) colder-colder (correcting tone and physical repositioning)" guidance until it becomes clear to him what it is you are asking him to do. Because you are not putting the stress on him to figure it out, but rather are showing him very plainly, he maintains his self-confidence and enjoys the activity.

If the dog is holding his position, your first amoeba-step can be followed by a second step, backing away from the dog with the left foot, With most dogs, it is better to take only that first step, draw the left foot up to a point even with the right so that there is a definite separation of 18 inches or so between the dog and you and hold that position for about one second. Then calmly, smoothly, but quickly step back to the dog, resuming your position next to his right shoulder. *Pause for another few second*, and then explode into praise-in-response (thereby releasing the dog from the command) which always includes petting, hugging, and even squealing (from you, not the dog).

Never praise the dog immediately upon returning to his shoulder. The dog must learn to wait calmly for the praise he knows is due him. This practice of waiting calmly for something he can hardly wait for gives him the opportunity to learn still more about being calm and controlling his body.

For a dog which tends to be hyperactive and have difficulty ever being calm, let your praise-in-response be very genuine but much quieter. Stroking instead of patting, and soothing praise instead of squeals will help the dog to remain in "thinking mode" for your next exercise.

When you put the dog on the **Sit-stay** command for the second time, you will often be able to take the second step, completing a separation of perhaps three to four feet between yourself and the dog. Always correct any mistake by giving the repositioning the dog. The correcting tone will reach your dog before your hands do, thus letting him know instantly that he has made a mistake. But emitting that tone is the *only* thing you do from a position remote from the dog. To reposition the dog, you must first return to him as quickly as possible (run!). Each time you repeat the **Sit-stay** exercise, the separation between you and the dog can increase by another step and the duration of the separation can increase by a few seconds.

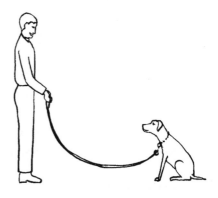

Leash-length SIT-STAY

When you are able to back up from the dog to the end of the leash, be very careful that you do not tug even slightly on the dog's collar with the leash. Keep your position frozen and the leash absolutely still and suspended with a little slack from your right hand. At this point, when you return to the position beside the dog's right shoulder, do so by walking back to him, passing along his left side and

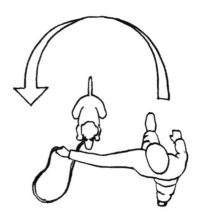

Returning from leash-length SIT-STAY

walking around behind him to come back up level with his right shoulder.

Occasionally, return to your dog in normal manner, pause, and then, instead of praising and releasing him, walk away again. This helps the dog learn that he is to remain in his position until you release him with praise-in-response, no matter how you behave around him and even if it looks to him like he ought to be through. This increases his ability to keep his concentration on the task at hand. It also teaches the owner that there is no need to repeat commands! No matter how many times you return to the dog and walk away again, if the dog is not released by the praise-in-response, he remains on command. The dog learns that he does not receive praise-in-response for having allowed you to return to him. He is praised for having held his position regardless of where you are, right next to him or in the next room, until you break the command. Dogs very clearly comprehend this.

One thing to be careful about when returning to your dog and leaving again: handle the leash very carefully. If you let the leash drape across the dog's back as you walk around him and back to his shoulder, then when you step away again, the leash is going to trail forward on his body. In the early stages of training this is almost certain to cause the dog to move. Always keep the leash from disturbing the dog in any way on a **Stay** exercise.

As your practice progresses, you can increase your distance from the dog still more. You can back to the end of the leash, lay the leash carefully on the ground, and continue adding steps to the distance between yourself and the dog. In this case, when returning to the dog, do not retrieve the leash. Leave it stretched out on the ground until you have released the dog from the command. There

Increasing distance for SIT-STAY

is too much movement of your body and the leash involved in

retrieving the leash, and it could invite the dog to make the mistake of moving.

Increase the duration of the **Sit-stay** incrementally until the dog can hold his position for about one minute. Normally, unless in a group situation where lots of interesting things are going on around the dog while he holds his **Sit-stay** position, I feel it is unfair to ask the dog to do a **Sit-stay** for longer than a minute or two. Boredom can set in, and the dog is entitled to get into a sleeping position if it is going to be a long wait for you!

Understand that the formal **Stay** command is not to be used for informal situations. An informal situation is one where the need is for the dog to remain within a certain general area (the yard, the car, etc.) while also being free to move about that area. For that need you can develop another phrase such as "wait here for me."

Only use the formal **Stay** command when you intend for the dog to remain unmoving in one precise spot, either sitting, lying down or standing, until you return. No matter how far you went away from your dog—even out of sight—always return to the **Heel** position before releasing him from the exercise.

The do's and don'ts for Sit-stay

DO NOT:

- Repeat the command word Stay.
- Scold or punish the dog for his mistakes.
- Expect the dog to fix his own mistakes.

DO:

- Drop your energy to zero to communicate stillness.
- Say the dog's name before the command word and hand signal.

- Step forward with your right foot but with no energy.
- Give the correcting tone if a mistake occurs and then fix the mistake.
- Give constant no-energy "praise-in-anticipation" by means of a big smile.
- Use "praise-in-response" to end the exercise.

Eight-week old puppy six days into dialogue!

CHAPTER 8

Down, But Not Out
(Down and Down-stay)

The **Down** exercise can be very simple for some dogs. For others it can pose a challenge. It seems that all dogs are either "standers" or "downers." Or something along the spectrum running between those two extremes. Very few fall right in the middle of this spectrum, enjoying both body positions equally.

To do the **Down** exercise, begin with your dog in the sitting position by your left side. Stoop, squat or kneel next to your dog, whatever gets you beside him and in a non-threatening position relative to him. Grasp the end of the collar, where it attaches to the leash, in your left hand. You should drop the leash at this point as there is no need for holding on to it. Position your right hand, palm down and fingers together, directly in front of the dog's nose. Give the command "Down" in a simple, declarative way, with neutral energy, neither harshly nor questioningly. The command should not be droned as was the **Stay** command. Furthermore, the command has a period after it, not a question mark nor an exclamation point. It is important that your tone of voice tells the dog that you are clear and calm about what you are doing and not excited or questioning! Simultaneously with the spoken command, the right hand should move directly downward to the ground. That is the hand signal and will always be part of the command even after the "training phase" is over.

To make this exercise happen for your dog, a split-second following the command word and hand signal, lower your left hand, the hand which is holding the end of the collar, to the ground. Keep firm hold of the collar, and literally pin the end of the collar to the ground with that hand. With profuse praise-in-anticipation, "talk the dog down." At first, the only thing you are doing to "make it happen" is lowering his head and neck. That is why it is so very

**Starting position for
hand signal for DOWN**

Making it happen

**Praise-in-response for
completed excercise**

important to keep the collar pinned to the ground no matter what. That lowering is the only indication to the dog of the direction you wish him to go and that you are praising him for going. At this point you simply want to get the dog's entire body on the ground within as few seconds as possible so that the dog gets his praise-in-response for a completed exercise. You can use the right hand, the signal hand, to pat the ground, or use it to stretch the dog's front legs out in front of him or push him off balance sideways—whatever works to get him down on the ground quickly and kindly. The dog will often even playfully pounce on your signal hand, thus cheerfully, even if unknowingly at first, moving in the correct direction!

With the collar pinned, it is fairly easy with most dogs to push them off balance, sometimes even with just the elbow of the left arm while the right hand is patting the ground. There are two reasons never to unpin the collar as you are positioning your dog. First, if you allow his head to rise up again, your dog loses all concept of what you are showing him to do and instead begins to think that you are interested in a fun wrestling match. The dog will be confused and will not learn. Bear in mind, to cause confusion is to be cruel. Secondly, you will never wrestle some large dogs to the ground successfully without pinning the collar unless you want to try a full body tackle. It is unlikely a dog will understand a body tackle at all, even if he ends up lying down under a handler's full weight. Besides, few handlers find such wrestling advisable.

Remember, the dog's neck is very muscular and cannot be hurt by pulling the collar downward. Your dog's feelings can be hurt, however. Without constant praise-in-anticipation, the dog might find this maneuver rather harsh and even frightening. But if you "talk him down" with constant, high-energy praise, he will feel that this action is all right with him. This is a classic example of the "hotter-hotter" part of the game. You cause the first move by the dog toward the ground by forcibly lowering his head, and immediately your voice tells him that he is heading in the correct direction. He will, to some degree, respond to that voice encouragement and continue in that direction—downward.

If the dog does not readily drop into the down position with your encouragement, do not fall into the trap of repeating the command. Praise-in-anticipation does *not* include repetition of **Down**. If the dog does not go down, it is *your* fault entirely, and giving the dog the command again (like the analogy with the math tutor) is not the answer. It is up to you to see to it that he "works the problem" correctly. If he does not lie down, it is because you did not put him into that position.

I referred earlier to the downer-stander spectrum. The effort it takes to put a dog into the **Down** position varies depending on where a dog falls on this spectrum. Those dogs at the far end of the "downer" side of the spectrum I call collapsible. Such a dog tends to take life primarily on his back with paws in the air. Take one look at him, and he hits the dirt. He is about as easy to move to a specific spot as cooked spaghetti. *But*, he picks up on the **Down** routine instantly! The only difficulty in teaching this type of dog any exercise is in getting him to wait for the command. Typically, you say his name, and he collapses.

If your dog does not hold the sitting position, but rather anticipates on his name and starts downward, this is a mistake that must simply be corrected just as any other mistake is corrected. Give the correcting tone and reposition your dog into the sitting position. Repeat his name, and if he waits for the command, then the command can be given. Such a correction is not only an opportunity for teaching the dog to be attentive when he hears his name, it also encourages him to become more emotionally stable so that he confidently waits for whatever command follows his name.

Under all circumstances, when he is so much as addressed by someone, the downer dog may prefer to roll over and ask for a tummy-rub, or, sadly, because he fears what may come next, to cringe to the ground. But with practice, even the downer dog learns instead to hold his sitting position until he has been given the next command. With the down exercise specifically, it is especially challenging for him to await the command when he sees you position your hands for the hand signal. He thinks it is coming, and he just can't wait! But he must wait because thereby he learns calmness and stability.

With any dog on the downer side of the spectrum, the job of putting him in the **Down** position will be accomplished very easily. Once the collar is pinned, if the dog has not yet dropped down, patting the ground with the signal hand after that hand has dropped downward always seems to do the trick. For a dog which falls in the middle of the downer/stander spectrum, often simply patting the ground, "talking him down" excitedly, and nudging him with the left elbow will be enough to get him into the down position.

The dedicated "standers" have quite a mental hangup with lying down. The stander must either think his joints do not close sufficiently to enable him to fold, or he finds it offensive to his self-image to have his body on the ground! Your dog's response to being put into the sitting position has already given you a hint as to his positioning on the downer/stander spectrum. As the handler, your attitude must not be affected by your dog's inclination to be a stander. You will, as with every exercise, "make it happen" so effectively that your dog is allowed to be oblivious to his shortcomings.

If the stander dog cannot hold the sitting position and wait for the **Down** command but rather stands up when he hears his name, correct him and return him to the sitting position. As I have explained before, the dog must learn that he is to be still and calm when he hears his name and await the command which he is learning always follows his name. He must not be allowed to anticipate or second-guess when he hears his name. In real life such behavior could be very dangerous for him.

Standers are the dogs which require all the acrobatics for getting them to the ground. If your dog happens to have "stander tendencies," use this procedure: While the collar is pinned and your praise mounts to a fever pitch, use your left elbow to push him off balance so that he falls over. If more effort is needed, your right hand, having completed the signal, can reach over and push the dog over, or gently pull the paws out, or even combine these efforts in some way. By whatever reasonable means, try to have the dog in the down position within a few seconds so that praise-in-response is not long in coming. The most determined stander will begin to fold on his own by about the fourth time of doing this exercise. The praise, he feels, is worth it!

No matter how you made it happen for your dog, as soon as your dog is all the way down, *release him completely* from the collar and your hands, elbow, whatever (he is not required to hold the position), and praise him profusely with hugging, petting and voice. Do not hold him in the down position, no matter how much effort it took to get him there. You are not waiting for glue to dry!

If your stander is one of the little breeds (stander behavior is common among poodles, for instance), I have found it gentler for the dog to simply be picked up in the right hand and laid on his side. The collar should still be pinned. The right hand can just pick the rest of the body up so as to remove the dog from his feet and lay him down on his side. If the collar is not pinned in the manner explained, the dog does not really get the sense that he is going down toward the ground from his sitting position. If the neck is lowered each time and the collar pinned, he learns that a response of going toward the ground is wanted. Putting him on his side just shows him the way to the prone position with the least pressure on the collar. The very small dogs, many of whom are of stander mentality, have very small necks, and this procedure will ensure that the collar exerts a harmless amount of pressure on their necks.

It is very important that you understand that it is perfectly fair to ask any dog to lie down. He is not being hurt either physically or emotionally. But he is learning this important thing—that when you ask him to do something, he must yield to your request even if he finds it distasteful. There will be times in his life when in order to survive in a human world, the dog may need to do things he finds uncomfortable or distasteful. He learns to yield to you, his interpreter in this society. The appreciation you give him he considers to be ample reward for overriding his self-will or misgivings.

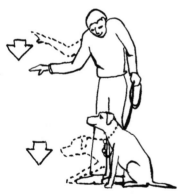

A recap: You must teach the dog how to respond to the command **Down** by *making it happen* over and over. The praise-in-anticipation is *so* important because without it the dog can be frightened by feeling his collar pinned to the ground. I have never

After sufficient practice, this dog now responds to command and hand signal for DOWN

frightened a dog with this procedure because my constant praise was sufficiently reassuring. Hearing my exuberant praise-in-anticipation, he is confident as always, and soon catches on to the purpose of the exercise as I repeatedly put him into the correct position.

Sometimes owners struggle with teaching themselves to praise a dog which is determinedly resisting moving downward. One owner even said, "I refuse to praise him if he isn't doing it." That owner missed the point that the dog *is* doing it if the owner is making it happen for him. Catch my concept. It works!

The **Down-stay** exercise is a simple step beyond the **Down**. When the dog has reached the lying down position, you do not break the command with praise-in-response. Instead, you immediately give the spoken command and hand signal for **Stay**, just as you would for the **Sit-stay** exercise. Just as with the **Sit-stay**, remember to give this command from a standpoint of zero energy, switching to the grin as the only praise-in-anticipation. You dropped the leash when first asking the dog to lie down, so it should still be on the ground. Do not pick it up. Upward movement with anything, even the end of the leash, could invite the dog to rise from his lying down position. Step away carefully, leading off with your right foot (remember, left foot for **Heel**, right foot for **Stay**), just as you did for the **Sit-stay** exercise.

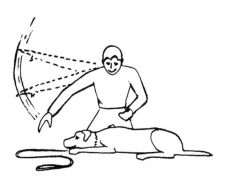

Early training position for giving command and hand signal for DOWN-STAY

If at any point your dog rises from his lying down position, give the correcting tone and reposition him, correcting his mistake. Use the collar primarily to reposition him, snapping down abruptly on it to return the dog to the lying down position. Use your hands only if

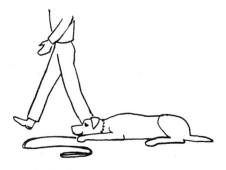

Step away with zero energy

you must push him off balance. If you use only your hands, without also using the collar, to correct his mistake, the dog can easily come to assume you are playing or wrestling. Pulling down on the collar triggers a memory of the movements you made to put him in the lying down position initially.

Remember, it is of no use to repeat the command **Stay**. Be aware, the dog is only making a mistake if he rises or moves away from where you asked him to stay. He can roll around or wriggle so long as he does not get up to so much as a sitting position, and so long as he does not wriggle or crawl away from the spot where you left him. Any movement away from that spot, even if he is still lying down, is a mistake. So also is rising to a sit or a stand, even if he does it on the spot where you left him.

To return to the dog after the **Down-stay**, you do just what you did to return after the **Sit-stay**. Walk to the right of the dog as you face him and around behind him, coming to a stop next to his right shoulder. The challenge for the dog is that he remain in the **Down** position when you return to him. If he gets up, even to a sitting position, give the correcting tone and reposition him. Any such behavior is a mistake that must be corrected by using the correcting tone and repositioning him.

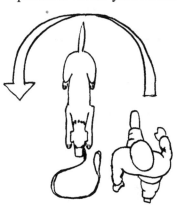

Return to HEEL position by going around behind dog

When you have returned to his right shoulder, the **Heel** position, you finish the exercise in this way before giving the dog praise-in-response: *[Warning: do not reach down and pick up the leash. As long as you do not stand on it when you return to the dog, it can just remain on the ground until the exercise is finished.]* Say your dog's name, and deliberately pause for a second or two to be sure the dog is not wanting to move on his name, perhaps second-guessing what is coming next. Stand tall and keep beaming that big grin (the praise-in-anticipation). Next, all the while standing very erect and

still, give the command **Sit** with a
burst of energy in your voice.
Immediately begin very energetic
praise-in-anticipation. If the dog
still remains in his lying down
position, pat your left thigh with
your left hand a few times. If the
dog still does not move, reach
down with your right hand and
jiggle upward on his collar while
continuing to praise and pat your
thigh.

Dog finishes to HEEL position

As soon as the dog rises to a sitting position, drop your energy
to zero (talking must stop) and stand absolutely still and erect,
grinning broadly. The drop in energy will indicate to the dog to
stop moving, and with a little luck he may freeze in a sitting
position next to you and look for all the world like the most highly
trained dog! You do not hold him responsible for that behavior at
this point, however. Just take note that if you were to keep your
high energy praise-in-anticipation going, he would follow that
energy with his behavior and proceed on from the sitting position
to standing to probably jumping up on you if you did not stop.
Simply stated, dogs respond to your energy. If the dog moves
beyond the sitting position, it is a mistake, and you correct it with
the correcting tone and reposition him sitting absolutely straight
beside your left leg, in the heel position. It is your responsibility to
exude no energy so that the dog thereby senses that he should stop
moving.

After a pause of at least a few seconds to be certain that the dog
is learning to wait calmly for his praise, explode into praise-in-
response for an exercise completed and well done! As with the **Sit-
stay** exercise, occasionally return to the dog, pause, and then walk
away again. Do not always finish the exercise (to the **Sit** position)
the first time you return to the dog.

Training should be life-saving if it is anything. Over time, the
Down-stay can become as long in duration, within reason, as you

want or need. ("Within reason" means not so long as to deprive the dog of necessary food and water or a chance to relieve himself!) It can be long enough to be truly life-saving, as it was for my dog, a very special German Shepherd named Aspen:

> It was an unusual November day with bright sunshine and temperatures in the 70's, abnormally balmy for late November in the high Rockies. Unable to resist the lure of the extraordinary day, I accepted an invitation for my family, which included my husband and young son, to take a hike. As there seemed no reason not to take Aspen along, we did so. Our friends had planned to hike in an area unfamiliar to my family, and the hike actually became somewhat of a rock-climbing activity as the trail wound around and over many huge boulders. Aspen, at age 12, still loved to hike, but his joints no longer took kindly to climbing over rocks. I helped lift his 90 pounds over all the obstacles, soon falling far behind my companions. I didn't care about them going on ahead as I was more interested in helping Aspen than in reaching any set destination. We reached one area from which I could see no way to keep moving upward with a 90-pound load. The others were by then long out of sight. I could not get Aspen any higher, and as I looked back in the direction from which we had come, I realized I could not get him back down without help either. He would have to be carried to descend from where we were. I needed to find my friends and family and ask their help. To do that, I would have to hike on alone and leave Aspen behind. But I knew that I could leave him on a Down-stay command and that he would wait confidently. I left him on command under a rock overhang that I could use as a landmark to return to since I could see that overhang from quite a distance.
>
> I hiked to the top of the trail, but my friends and family were nowhere to be seen. It seemed the only logical next step was to return to our car and wait for the return of the hiking party. It was now late afternoon. It *was* November, and the sun would soon drop from sight. Despite the summer-like afternoon, I knew that at that altitude the temperature would plunge as soon as the sun set. The night would be very long and cold. At his

age, Aspen would not fare well in the elements overnight. We had to get him back home.

Just before sunset, I heard voices coming down the trail. I ran to meet my friends and family and informed them that we had to go back up and get Aspen. My friends simply didn't believe me when I said the dog would be waiting, expecting us to return for him. They suggested that I just go part way back up the trail and call for him. But I explained that he was nearly deaf, so calling would do no good. They said he would probably find his way back down in due time by himself, but I countered that besides being no longer able to climb down over rocks, he was also nearly blind. It had been more than two hours, and they were sure that Aspen would have wandered somewhere by then and returning to that overhang would be a waste of time and energy. Besides, it would soon be dark, and no one wanted to be hiking in the dark. At this point my husband broke off the argument abruptly and said to me, "Let's go." *He* knew Aspen was trained to hold a stay for however long it was asked of him. He knew he would be there, patiently waiting under the overhang.

And so he was. He had not moved an inch. Our reunion was happy, but Aspen treated it all matter-of-factly. After all, he had had no notion that he had been abandoned as he had learned through his lifetime that I always returned to him to complete a Stay exercise. We carried him down to safety and home, *very* grateful that our beloved dog had this life-saving training in place.

The do's and don't's for Down and Down-stay

DO NOT:

- Repeat any commands.
- Expect the dog to remain down for an indefinite period unless given the command Stay.
- Scold or punish the dog for his mistakes.
- Expect the dog to fix his own mistakes.

DO:

- Say the dog's name before the command and hand signal for Down.
- Give energetic "praise-in-anticipation" as you position the dog.
- Drop your energy to zero before giving the command Stay.
- Give the correcting tone if a mistake occurs and then fix the mistake.
- Give constant, low-energy "praise-in-anticipation" by means of a big smile.
- Return the dog to the Heel position before ending the exercise.
- Use "praise-in-response" to end the exercise.

CHAPTER 9

Statue-like
(Stand and Stand-stay)

It is possible you will not appreciate the utility of the **Stand-for-examination** (**Stand-stay**) exercise until you take your dog to the groomer's or the veterinarian's. But sooner or later you will have a chance to use the exercise in real life. (It is a wonderful at-home grooming aid!) The daily practice of this exercise teaches your dog great powers of concentration and self-control, qualities which will spill over into all his other behavior. For this exercise he must learn to focus on four points (his four feet) and keep them from moving in any way at all. That is quite a step up from holding a down-stay which allows for shifting and rolling.

To do this exercise, start with the dog sitting beside your left leg (in the **Heel** position), just as you have with the other formal exercises. To begin the **Stand-for-examination**, stoop or kneel beside your dog unless your dog is larger than you and is likely to push you off balance,. Grasp the dog's collar at the point where the leash attaches. If you are in a location that is safe for the dog, unsnap the leash and set it aside. It is not needed, and it actually can be a nuisance. The starting position for the hand signal is identical with the **Down** exercise.

Once you grasp the dog's collar and position your right hand palm down and fingers together directly in front of his nose, you will probably find out whether your dog thinks he's a "downer" or a "stander" (as discussed in Chapter 8). The downer wants you to give the **Down** command, and he just as fervently hopes that you are *not* going to give the **Stand** command. He further anticipates that by jumping the gun when you say his name, he will get to do the exercise he prefers—that is, the **Down**. The anticipatory response of the stander dog when he sees the hand positions and hears his name is equal but opposite. He wants to jump to the **Stand** position, the exercise he prefers. In either case, anticipating the

**Early training position
for giving command and
hand signal for STAND**

**After hand signal, bring dog to his
feet and transfer collar to right hand**

**Release collar and steady
dog on both hands**

command is a mistake. Give the correcting voice tone and reposition the dog.

When the dog is willing to sit and wait for the command, say the command **Stand** with a moderate amount of energy—less than for **Heel**, but more than for **Down**. Then move your right hand parallel with the ground away from the dog's nose. Tug forward on the collar with your left hand. Pull the collar forward until it meets up with the right hand. Transfer the collar to your right hand. All this should bring the dog to his feet unless he is totally collapsible, in which case he will already be on his back. No matter. You are obligated to make it happen for him, to stand him on his feet while giving him lavish praise-in-anticipation. Your left hand is now free to be placed under the dog, in front of the hind legs. This hand both holds the dog so that he doesn't leap away and steadies him in the standing position. If the dog is flat out on the ground, the left hand and arm can reach under him and lift him to his feet. Remember to be "talking him into position" with praise-in-anticipation.

As soon as the dog is standing fairly steadily, supported by your left hand, your right hand must *release the collar* and assume a position of support under the dog's jaw. (Any jingling or tugging of the collar would work at cross purposes with the effort to put the dog in a standing position. The dog has learned to associate even just a jingle of the collar with assuming a sitting position.)

Steady the dog with your hands only so that the dog stands apart from your body completely by a foot or more. Once the dog is steadied on your two hands as I described above, one under the back half of his belly and the other under his jaw, you must drop your energy to zero, which means you must stop giving that verbal praise-in-anticipation. A grin is optional because the dog is not usually looking back over his shoulder at you since your right hand is encouraging his head to stay straight. Technically, his head is allowed to move, but it is a rare dog that can swing his head very far without a foreleg following. It is better to steady the dog's head straight forward because it makes it easier for him to hold all four feet still.

As you are positioning your dog in the **Stand** and praising with your voice, guard against the temptation to use those positioning hands inadvertently to rub his tummy! It is almost a subconscious move. If the voice is praising, the hands want to pet. But that would be praise-in-response and would break the command.

Once the dog is standing squarely and steadily, remove your hands from the dog about one inch, just enough so that you know, and the dog knows, you are no longer holding him steady. In the beginning you shoot for "one inch for one second." If the dog remains immobile for one or two seconds, he gets praise-in-response. To praise him, simply move your hands back up the inch to his tummy and jaw and rub away! Don't take time to lift your arm up and over his back in order to give him a hug. Praising from underneath is more immediate and it reinforces in his mind that he is being praised for standing. In the time it takes you to lift your arm over his back, the dog could move one of his feet, and you would therefore be praising a mistake. The dog is only required to hold stock still for a second or two, but you want to praise that successful effort.

Hands completely off dog

**Give praise -in-response
from underneath**

If, while you are attempting to withdraw your hands one inch, the dog moves in any way (and he may move in *many* ways), just use the correcting tone sharply so that he knows there has been a mistake, and quickly and precisely position him again with the two hands, one under his belly and the other under his jaw. Then slowly and carefully withdraw the hands one inch again. You have to be very alert on this exercise to notice any and all movement so that you correct the mistakes and do not reward movement. The dog has multiple places to keep still, giving you multiple places to watch and correct!

After sufficient practice the dog will be able to hold the **Stand** position perfectly while you take your hands farther away, and eventually back to your lap, for several seconds. Always be alert to correct mistakes. The farther away you take your hands, the more challenging it is to correct a mistake at the moment it is made and before the dog has moved totally out of position. When the dog seems very solid and steady with standing still, slowly rise to a standing position next to him.

Step by step with practice the dog will get better at holding still, and you can eventually give him the command (word and hand) for the **Stay** exercise and carefully step away from him. Do not have the leash attached when doing **Stand-stay**. You must always have your body cocked and ready to drop down next to him to correct any mistakes. You cannot correct mistakes in the dog's **Stand** from a standing position yourself. You would have to bend over the dog, and the average dog will not want to stand up if you are bending over him. All mistakes must be corrected (his body repositioned) from underneath and without using the collar.

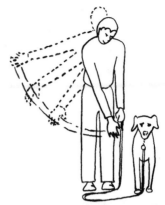

Position for giving command and hand signal for STAND-STAY

Recall that this exercise is called the **Stand-for-examination**. The final step is for another person to walk up to the dog as he is holding his **Stand-stay** with you standing a few feet away from him. This person should be able to look him all over, check his teeth, pat his rump, and gently do whatever he wants without the dog moving or showing fear or hostility. You can see how important this exercise can be for rehabilitating a problem dog that has snapped at people because of his fear and confusion.

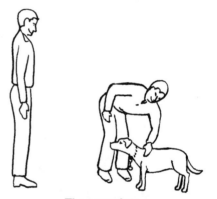

The complete STAND-FOR EXAMINATION

At this point, you can complete the whole exercise all the way through the "finish" to the **Heel** position. To do this "finish," return to the dog just as you have on both the **Sit-stay** and **Down-stay**, by passing to the right of the dog (as you face him) and walking behind him and back up alongside his right side. You must do this very carefully at first, being ever ready to correct the almost inevitable mistake the dog will make when he sees you walk up next to his right shoulder. He will feel he should assume a sitting position as soon as you are standing in the customary **Heel** position beside him. Correct this mistake if it occurs. By learning to concentrate on his **Stand-stay** and wait for you to ask for the next thing, your dog will be increasing his attentiveness and ability to focus.

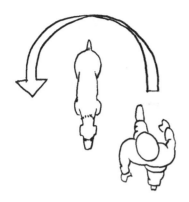

Return to dog after STAND-STAY

**Couple steps of HEEL
finishes exercise**

**HEEL always finishes
to sitting position**

Furthermore, as with the **Sit-stay** and **Down-stay**, the dog will learn he is not through with the **Stand-stay** just because you return to the **Heel** position beside him. You may return to that position and then walk away again before deciding to finish the exercise.

When you are ready to finish to the **Heel** position, all that is needed is for you to say the dog's name, give the command **Heel,** and then step forward with the left foot. One or two steps are sufficient to get your dog to move forward from his frozen standing position. When you stop after that step or two, he will automatically (after sufficient practice of the **Heel** exercise) assume a sitting position next to your left leg. He does not need to learn anything new to do the finish for this the **Stand-stay**. But until your dog knows to sit automatically when you halt from the **Heel,** say his name and the command **Sit** and put him in place.

I have used this **Stand-for-examination** exercise in so many ways. Veterinarians, of course, are delighted to examine a dog that will hold still. It is a godsend for x-rays. I have used this exercise countless times in rehabilitating abused and traumatized dogs which were afraid to let any stranger approach them.

On this command, a dog can override his flight impulse and allow a person to approach him and pet him. Over time the flight impulse can become greatly subdued so that a previously fearful dog can tolerate strangers' presence even when not on a **Stand-stay** command.

Even with some dogs which are not afraid of people, the **Stand-stay** is a most effective way to introduce the dogs to strangers. If a dog is big, people like to be able to pet such a dog without wondering if the dog will do something unpleasant to them. Of course, a trained dog would not do something impulsive and unpleasant, but the general public does not yet know much about trained dogs. My best memory of using the Stand-stay exercise is from my own dog Tippy:

> Tippy had been so brutally abused prior to her rescue that she needed immense rehabilitation. I used the Stand-stay exercise for two years as the only way strangers could get close to her. Then one day I took her to a groomer for a bath. The groomer first wanted to trim Tippy's nails. Tippy was quite terrified to be up on that metal table with the groomer trying to hold up one of her paws. I foolishly hugged Tippy and tried through sheer comforting talk to help her to be able to hold still. It was hopeless. Then a light bulb lit in my mind, and I remembered that Tippy had her comfort zone, her Toastmaster's Club, to help her. I put her on a **Stand-stay** command on that table, and she was immediately calm, unmoving, and allowed the groomer to lift one paw after the other and trim the nails. Tippy was able to totally override her fears in order to respond to a command.

Dialogue certainly makes life easier for Tippy. It has actually given her a happy life. And such happy endings occur over and over again every day and everywhere for dogs which are given the chance to learn to live in a constant dialogue with their human partners.

The do's and don't's for Stand and Stand-stay

DO NOT:

- Repeat any commands.
- Scold or punish the dog for his mistakes.
- Expect the dog to fix his own mistakes.

DO:

- Say the dog's name before the command word and hand signal for Stand.
- Give energetic "praise-in-anticipation" as you position the dog.
- Work only from beside and under the dog, not above and over the dog.
- Drop your energy to zero before giving the command Stay.
- Give the correcting tone if a mistake occurs and then fix the mistake.
- Give constant, low-energy "praise-in-anticipation" by means of a big smile.
- Return the dog to the Heel position before ending the exercise.
- Use "praise-in-response" to end the exercise.

CHAPTER 10

Come to Me
(Recall)

Even though your dog should be learning that he only investigates things in company with you, there may be those times when for some reason the two of you are separated by some distance. Perhaps you are on a hike, and in that instance the 'informal walk" is allowing the still attentive dog to run large circles around you to burn up excess energy. Should a need arise for the dog to be immediately with you, the dog needs to have learned to return to you instantaneously, and preferably with the speed of a bullet, when you request it. If you know your dog has learned as a body reflex to literally do a back-flip and fly back to you when he hears the command **Come,** you can be confident that your dog is safe in nearly every situation.

> A student told me of a time when her dog alerted her to the presence of a bear at the back end of her yard. The medium-sized dog was approaching the bear, barking, following an impulse to protect its home and yard. The owner, however, knew that the valiant dog would be no match for an irritated bear. She yelled the dog's name and the command **Come,** and the dog, without a second's hesitation, turned around and raced back to her. The owner was so thrilled and relieved that she had to phone me immediately to share the story.

Another student e-mailed her account of a little experience to me:

> We had a very good test case the other night when I stepped outside with Sizzle, my Sheltie, before going to bed. She suddenly dashed up the hill, and I heard a deer taking off. I called out, and she stopped in her tracks immediately. Wow.

Occasionally there may be a situation when response to **Stay** is life-saving, as with my dog Aspen. But the recall (**Come**) has undeniably been the exercise which has saved the most dogs.

To begin teaching your dog the recall, or **Come** exercise, give your dog the **Sit-stay** command and step to the end of the leash just as you do for the **Sit-stay** exercise. Wear that huge grin and carefully keep a frozen body position. Quietly say the dog's name. The dog must learn that he is not to move on his name, just as he is not to anticipate any other command when he first hears his name. By keeping your voice quiet and devoid of energy when saying your dog's name, your dog will sense that he is to remain still.

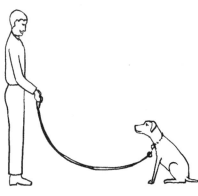

RECALL begins from a SIT-STAY position

Slowly count to five silently while watching for any sign of movement from the dog. Any movement must be instantaneously corrected as with any **Sit-stay** exercise.

Keep your own body in a frozen position, just as you do for any **Stay** command. The dog reads all your body English, and if you were to make even a slight move—to bend toward him or reach toward the leash or even suddenly suck in a big breath of air in anticipation of the command you are about to give—he would read that action as an invitation to move toward you. With some dogs it is almost as if there is a rubber band being stretched between dog and handler when the handler walks away, leaving the dog on his **Sit-stay**. When the dog hears his name preparatory to the command, his desire to second-guess that it will be a **Come** command makes him

Make it happen by reeling the dog in to you

feel as if the rubber band is stretched to the breaking point. Any movement on your part would in effect release the rubber band. So, hold your frozen position until it is apparent to you that the dog is solidly holding his position and waiting for further direction.

Put dog into sitting position facing you

Then, and only then, say the command **Come** with all the energy and enthusiasm you can put into that one word and immediately move to "make it happen." A split second after giving the command, snap on the leash much as you would give a snap on a fishing line if you sensed a fish was nibbling at the bait. Then, to continue the fishing analogy, quickly and with a sense of urgency "reel" the dog in to you by hand-over-hand taking up the leash until the dog is directly in front of you, his nose nearly

Waiting patiently for further instructions

touching your legs. Then very quickly put him into the sitting position facing you.

No other commands are given after the initial **Come**, but very, very energetic praise-in-anticipation is given the dog all the while he is on his way to you and into the sitting position. Be alert that you do not inadvertently pet the dog with your hands as you put him into the **Sit** in front of you. It is so easy to do so without thinking because your voice is giving constant praise.

As soon as the dog is sitting, stand up straight, hands off the dog, voice now quiet. Be looking down at the dog with that huge grin lighting up your face. Pause for a few seconds. Insist that the dog remain sitting quietly, and correct him by giving him a correcting tone and placing him back in position if he does not. Then, after a few quiet seconds, explode into praise-in-response with hugs and pats and petting.

Practice this exercise always on leash for the first 100 or more times. Remember, you are teaching your dog a body reflex, not a cerebral response. (A dog is a thinking creature, yes, but in a life-threatening situation, he may not have time to think.) If the command **Come** is followed by the dog being moved toward you with great immediacy and speed over and over again (and you will see to it that this is what happens), in due time the dog will jump up and move toward you as if on automatic pilot when he hears the command **Come**.

At some point, after much practice on leash, if you judge that the dog is responding very well because he runs to the position in front of you faster than you can reel in the leash, try the exercise off leash. Unsnap the leash and carry it in your hand as you leave the dog on the **Sit-stay**. For the first try, only go as far as the end of the leash would be if it were attached. If the dog responds with immediacy to the command, go a little farther away the next time. If the dog does not respond immediately to the command, rev up the praise-in-anticipation that you are using and, for this extra encouragement only, pat your thighs with your hands. If the dog still does not respond, or if he starts toward you and then moves off the straight line to you and begins to seek out some other diversion, this is what you must do: run to him, grab the end of his collar, and pull him with you *as you run backward* to the spot where you were standing when you called him. Use praise-in-anticipation non-stop the entire time. When he is sitting in front of you calmly, end the exercise with praise- in-response.

By following this procedure, you have seen to it that your dog completed the exercise, and he gets all the credit for a perfect performance. However, the next time you do this exercise, do it on leash! Practice many more times on leash for several practice sessions until you feel you should check out the progress again off leash.

Because all formal exercises begin from the **Heel** position, it is convenient to 'finish" all exercises to this position before you give praise-in-response. And it is very simple for you to finish all but one of the exercises (the recall or **Come**) that way. To finish the recall exercise to the **Heel** position is a little more complicated. I will explain this unique "finish" as a separate exercise.

To have your dog finish to the **Heel** position from his sitting position in front of you, the dog does not need to learn anything new. Place the dog a **Sit** in front of you. Say his name and the command **Heel.** Have the leash in your right hand adjusted to the length for a normal **Heel** exercise. Take a step *backward* with your right foot. Your dog should be comfortable with moving forward upon hearing the command **Heel** and will only need a slight movement of the leash hand to the right of your body to reassure him that he can move forward alongside your right leg. Your right leg, since it is next to him, is the one the dog expects to move with. It does not bother him at all that you are walking backward.

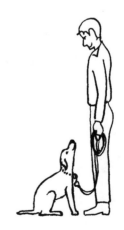

Dog has just completed RECALL

As soon as your dog is heeling confidently, urged on by much praise-in-anticipation, stop walking backward and take several steps forward. The dog will without hesitation move around

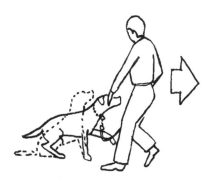

Heeling backward

**Reversing direction of the heeling
(dog executes an about-face)**

Halting from HEEL

your back and proceed, heeling, now next to your left leg. That is because your dog is primarily watching your legs moving first in one direction and then in the opposite direction. From his point of view, he perceives that you have just done an about-face even though you have not. Now that you are walking forward, you then move on however many steps are needed to return to the exact same spot from which you began, the spot on which your dog had been sitting originally.

The number of steps taken backward will diminish with practice until you only need to move your right leg to encourage your dog to rise from his sitting position following the command **Heel** and move forward and around your body to a position alongside your left leg. Eventually, your dog will respond completely to the command **Heel** and not need any effort on your part (no leg movement) to "make it happen." He will rise from the sitting position facing you, pass around behind you from your right side to your left side, and resume sitting, now in the **Heel** position. He is then on the **Heel** command and knows to hold his **Sit** until further instructions are given or the command is broken with praise-in-response.

The goal of the recall is for the dog to immediately turn from whatever he is doing and run with urgency to his owner, stop, assume a sitting position in front of his owner (no **Sit** command needed), and await further instructions. By facing the owner in this way, the dog is most attentive to the next communication, if such is needed. However, frequent practice of the recall, followed by a finish to the **Heel** position each time, would soon have the dog combining the two (recall and finish) in his mind and responding to the command **Come** by returning to the owner and going directly to the **Heel** position. The **Come** followed immediately by the finish should be reserved for exhibition purposes only.

To recap: In order to execute the "finish to the **Heel** position" after the **Come** exercise, the dog does not initially need to learn any responses new to him. The only one who has to learn new tricks with this exercise is you! Think it through and practice by yourself before trying this with your dog. It is simpler than most people want to make it. A few steps straight back followed by a few steps straight forward to the point from which backward steps began are all that is required.

The do's and don't's for the recall

DO NOT:

- Allow the dog to anticipate and move on its name.
- Repeat the command word Come.
- Scold or punish the dog for his mistakes.
- Expect the dog to fix his own mistakes.

DO:

- Say the dog's name quietly and carefully during the training period.

- Remain frozen in position and count to at least five before giving the command Come.
- Bring the dog to you as fast as possible and put the dog immediately into a sitting position in front of you.
- Give energetic praise-in-anticipation non-stop until the dog is sitting in front of you.
- Freeze with only a smile for low-energy praise for at least several seconds while the dog holds his position.
- Give the correcting tone if a mistake occurs and then fix the mistake.
- Use "praise-in-response" to end the exercise.

Basic method reminders

Refer to all parts of this book often, as the philosophy expressed herein is foundational to working with your dog in a precise way, the way he would most like you to do it and the way it is most effective. I am well aware that the very detailed and specific procedures that comprise my method may seem unnecessarily fussy. However, over the years I have found that when my students compromised precision, the dogs did not learn the exercises as quickly or as well. Impatience with the precision resulted in a weaker dialogue. And the degradation of the dialogue meant some degree of uncertainty and insecurity for the dog.

Here is a summary of the do's and don't's that are fundamental to this philosophy:

1. Say the dog's name before each and every command. Do not randomly repeat his name during your conversation.

2. Never let the dog move on his name. Always pause, even if only slightly, between name and command to ensure the dog waits for his instructions. To wait for instructions could be the most life-saving thing he learns!

3. Never repeat commands.

4. Follow every command with "praise-in-anticipation" non-stop (your conversation).

5. Complete a formal exercise before giving "praise-in-response," that is, the praise with petting and fuss which breaks the command.

6. First practice each new exercise by yourself, without your dog.

7. Be alert so your reaction time becomes split-second.

8. Develop calmness in yourself; the dog can then learn calmness.

9. Backwash success from an exercise that a dog does easily to an exercise that he does reluctantly. In other words, always end your practice on a good note!

10. Never allow friends or relatives to "check out your dog's training" by giving him commands—they do not know the language. It is rude for people to presume that they can do that, but you cannot always control your friends, and especially your relatives. Some of them just do not know they are overstepping their bounds. Intervene in some diplomatic way or quietly and gently move the dog to another location!

PHOTO MOMENT

Undisturbed by the visitor

SECTION III

SEEING THE BIGGER PICTURE

CHAPTER 11

Moral Commitment

Some statistics indicate that 80 percent of dogs dropped at pounds and shelters in the United States are abandoned because of behavior problems. Make no mistake—"giving up" a dog to a shelter is abandonment. Even though the deed is not done along the side of the road, it still qualifies as abandonment. Other sources say that abandonment, both on roadsides and in institutions, is increasing. Because there are simply not enough adoptive homes available, abandonment, even to shelters, means death for the dog in a majority of cases. This death is an indescribable horror, but William W. Forgey, M.D. paints a vivid picture:

> "It has to still be dreadful to face death, even in the reassuring arms of your human friend. But what a horror to be stored with terrified others, to be shoved into a chamber and to have the air sucked out of your lungs, or to be injected with air, or potassium chloride, or sodium pentothal by an uncaring or at least an indifferent executioner while still at your prime while you are still filled with the God-given innate will to live and to thrive. It's an unimaginable fate except for those who have been subjected to a human holocaust." (from the Foreword to *Dog Adoption* by Joan Hustace Walker)

Often when a dog is abandoned for behavior problems, the owner replaces the abandoned dog with a new puppy. People in general do not understand dog behavior and what is causing that behavior which to them appears to be "bad." They think the problem lies with the dog and can be eliminated by replacing the dog. After all, that is what we do if we have a vehicle which turns out to be a lemon. This pattern—abandonment and replacement—fuels puppy production nationwide. The result is more and more dogs and not enough homes.

To make matters worse, the statistics already stated are giving shelter dogs a bad rap. Since the majority of shelter dogs are considered by many people to have a history of problem behavior, you have a stage set for mass destruction of unwanted dogs. Because shelter dogs are thought to have unredeemable behavior problems, there are not millions of people willing to adopt these millions of dogs presently in shelters and needing homes. Meanwhile, more puppies, all of which need homes, are constantly being produced.

There is no doubt spaying and neutering of dogs is necessary to curb puppy production. But the abandonment issue is equally important, and it must be addressed. Every effort needs to be made to *keep* dogs in their homes and families for their life span. Dogs deserve the stability such continuity of home and companionship affords. Quick, effective, loving and enjoyable dialogue-based training can cure, or prevent the development of, behavior problems. Therefore, such training is *the* most important effort aimed at preventing abandonment. Society needs *that* solution to the growing number of homeless dogs. If we do not solve the behavior problems, destruction of millions of dogs every year remains the only practical alternative.

Joan Hustace Walker writes in *Dog Adoption*:

> "Rarely is there a behavioral problem that can't be corrected with a little time, patience, and the correct modification training. When you adopt an adult dog from a shelter, remember that the same problems that existed before the dog came to the shelter are now your problems. The difference is that you are willing to work with your dog and make him into a model canine citizen."

Decades of experience have proven for me that dogs can be adopted with confidence from a shelter. Adoptive owners can learn to dialogue with their dogs and thereafter help their dogs live successfully according to the rules of human society. Dog owners who are presently faced with what is considered "bad" behavior by their dogs can learn WR-DOS and thereby solve those problems.

Then these owners can fulfill their commitment to provide lifetime care for their dogs. Abandonment should not be an option.

There are only two reasons why, when faced with "bad" dog behavior, an owner cannot keep his commitment to the puppy or dog for which he has become guardian: (1) He does not know the way to help his dog change his behavior patterns. 2) He cannot be bothered to help his dog change. A dog owner is deprived of the first reason for breaking his commitment when he reads this book. This book has explained, in a way that any dog owner can understand, the "dog problem" in this country (abandonment and subsequent destruction). A dog owner also has learned from this book the fact that there *are* training solutions. Therefore, he has no moral justification for abandoning his dog. The second reason, indifference, is totally unacceptable. Anyone who does not care about the well-being of his dog should not have acquired a dog in the first place.

Adoption of a dog needs to be seen as a serious, long-term commitment. We live in a "throw-away" society, but living beings must never be classified as throw-aways. Countless concerned volunteers and donors are having to provide millions of hours and millions of dollars to try to deal with the millions of homeless dogs in the United States alone. It is ethically unjustifiable for someone to renounce his commitment to a dog and expect "someone else" to step in and assume responsibility for that dog.

The training concepts of WR-DOS have proven to be particularly effective in eliminating behavioral problems. Furthermore, the procedures are relatively quick and easy for dog owners to learn and practice. For these reasons, WR-DOS can have an especially significant impact on the problem of dog abandonment. Obviously, however, to make this impact, the information contained in this book must be widely broadcast through every available avenue. Please share the knowledge you have gained from this book as widely as you can.

My hope is that someone on the staff of every shelter will learn WR-DOS and use it to improve the adoption possibilities for every dog in his or her care. Initiating dialogue with shelter dogs and working with them so as to begin to restore their confidence and self-esteem would be a big step toward the goal of 100 percent adoption rates. Following adoption, new owners can then learn WR-DOS from the shelter staff, from someone else who has learned WR-DOS sufficiently to teach it, or from this book. An owner's conscientious training efforts will do much to ensure a successful, permanent relationship between himself and his dog.

We can reduce the number of dogs abandoned because of behavior problems. Shelters can then devote their time and resources to caring for the dogs who have actually lost their homes due to natural disasters or because of the incapacitation or death of their human partners. Let us work toward the goal of "every dog in a responsible home to stay."

CHAPTER 12

For a Better World

One of the premises of this book is that dogs deserve something far better than domination. They deserve a dialogue with humans who are appreciative of their unique identities and sensitive to their needs. When humans fail to make the effort to understand their dogs' personalities and their individual concerns, the dogs always suffer. Listen to what another caring owner tells of his dog's need for an understanding home:

Coco is a chocolate-brown female Sharpei. We got Coco from the local animal shelter. The shelter had little information on Coco's past. The only information they gave us was that she had come to the shelter from a town about 25 miles away.

We started her and ourselves in WR-DOS training. About a week later, a mail carrier from Coco's town of origin saw her and recognized her. She told us Coco had been well known for being very aggressive and possibly vicious. She had lived in at least two different homes. The postal service in her town would not deliver mail to either of those homes if she was out because she was judged to be dangerously aggressive. This woman was amazed that Coco did not appear to any longer be aggressive or vicious.

The WR-DOS training has been very beneficial for both Coco and us, her "family." Through the time spent with Coco in our practice sessions, Coco and we have gotten to know each other better. We understand what is expected of dog and owner in our relationship. As a result of the training, we have developed a mutual respect and trust. We have never observed in Coco the aggressive behavior she was known for in her past. We feel Coco's past is now behind her. When we have houseguests, we have no concerns about Coco's behavior or our visitors' safety. Coco enjoys being the center of attention.

Coco, like the majority of dogs I meet, had no self-confidence when we began working with her. But each dog needs to be respected as a unique personality and treated as such. Coco needed some very specific things to help her to feel confident and at peace. I keep Coco in my home occasionally when her owners travel. Her behavior tells quite a story. It took us awhile to experiment and come up with the situation in which she felt happiest in our home. Most dogs are not that particular, but from this need to find the "just right" situation for Coco in our home, we learned something about her. If Coco were a person, she might be called a crotchety old lady. To support her feeble confidence, she requires everything around her to be "just so." She is very happy staying in a room of our house which has pens along one wall with dog doors giving access from the pens to a yard. She is not happy closed out of the room, outside the dog door, with the dog door latched shut. Neither is she happy in the room with the dog door latched shut. She is very content and happy in the room only if the dog door is open to her, even though she doesn't like to spend much time outdoors.

Coco communicates these things to us very easily because we take the time and interest to watch her and take note of how she responds to alternative situations. We notice both when she is peaceful and when she is fretful. Coco not only needs the confidence-building communication with people which WR-DOS affords her, she needs a very precisely tailored living environment because she is basically a worry-wart! Progress is evident each time she stays with us.

If a dog has a delicate or temperamental personality makeup and is in a home where he is run over rough shod by the human inhabitants, his behavior is likely to reflect his increasing worry, confusion, and frustration. If he is then punished for that undesirable behavior, his behavior problems will be compounded. Aggression and timidity are very often opposite sides of the same coin. In Coco's case, her "viciousness" was merely her way of crying out her need for a comforting, encouraging, secure, and precisely ordered environment. But her vicious behavior could have cost her her life. I'm glad this story had a happy-ever-after ending.

Above all, learn to appreciate your dog's intelligent individuality. Dogs are not unfeeling playthings. Respect their sensitivity and perceptiveness. If you have a friend or relative who insists on giving your dog commands to "check out how school is going," find another place to leave your dog when that person comes to call. You cannot always get people to show proper respect for your dog, but you can shelter your dog from this kind of ignorant abuse. Do the same if someone who dislikes or resents dogs comes to your home. Dogs are so much more sensitive than most humans, but even with our relative insensitivity, we all know what it feels like to be in the presence of someone who dislikes us. It is not a positive, progressive experience for us to be with someone who does not respect us or who resents us, so do not force it on your dog.

It is their sensitivity and ability to read the atmosphere, so to speak, that makes dogs behave in uncanny, intuitive ways. That is why living with a dog is so interesting and rewarding. Books are filled with true stories of dogs warning their owners of danger or sensing when a family member is in need. Dogs express their intelligence in marvelous ways, and the more we develop our communication with them and appreciate their intelligence, the more we can benefit from our relationship with them.

It is a fast-paced, hectic world. If the dogs are going to survive at all, we humans are going to have to slow down and listen to what they are telling us with their actions. We must not be so quick to label the dogs as stubborn, stupid, defiant, dominant, aggressive or mean. We must take time to become acquainted with their individual personalities and meet their needs for not only surviving but thriving in this human world—a world in many ways so alien for dogs. The whole process of developing a dialogue with one's dog provides a uniquely effective way to do this. We will be abundantly repaid for our efforts.

One of the chief benefits my students and I have derived from working with dogs is an enlarged understanding of human behavior. I am indebted to Coco, Breeze, Rajah, Yogi, Klansey and a host of other problem-ridden dogs who have taught me so much about *people*. They have taught me to look beyond appearances to find the root causes of the unacceptable behavior I witness in human beings.

It is such a joy for me to have a student come up to me and say, as many have done, "I'm learning so much about people from this work with my dog." One student, an administrator at a nursing home, shared this insight which she had gained after only a few days of helping her dog, a dog which she had rescued from an abusive past:

> L.H. is an elderly woman who is in the nursing facility where I work. She can't see very well, can't hear very well, and is restricted to a wheelchair. She is not at all pleasant to be around because she is angry all the time. Any staff member attempting to take care of her will most assuredly be berated at some time or another. Because of this, many staff tend to her physical needs but will avoid nurturing her emotional needs with a hug, or a smile, or maybe a conversation. Housekeeping staff come into her room to clean it when she's not there to avoid meeting up with her. If she discovers someone has been in her room in her absence, she will assume someone was trying to steal something from her. She can't understand why she has to wake up in the middle of the night to find strangers in her room (when the nurses come in to take care of her).
>
> She was mistreated as a child, then as a wife. She took care of herself all of her life and now is dependent upon others. Her experience all of her life has been that others don't take very good care of her, so this frightens her.

> She cannot understand that her anger is contributing
> to her loneliness. What is saddest of all is that the root
> of her anger is her fear of being mistreated.

When this student shared this with me, I responded by saying, "Isn't it a good thing that euthanasia of humans isn't legal? If it were, this woman, like so many dogs, would not be allowed to live." My student replied, "But to be cut off from all love as she is, is a kind of death." True.

Let's learn from the dogs.

We can learn that bad behavior does not mean that the individual is bad.

We can learn that much of the "mud" that is hiding our true colors was plastered on to us by society's labeling.   In the introduction to her book *Real Lives: Eleven Teenagers Who Don't Go to School*, author Grace Llewellyn makes a very perceptive statement about those young people society calls school "dropouts."

> "To some degree, we all fulfill others' expectations of
> us, and kids who call themselves dropouts cannot help
> but absorb—to at least some degree—society's
> pessimistic judgments on their capabilities and futures."

We can learn that the mud is not a permanent part of us.

We can learn that it is okay to be wrong sometimes, and that we can learn from our mistakes.

We can learn that we all deserve to hear that we are good, and that someone believes we can do the right thing, albeit perhaps with a little help.

We can learn that no one should have to reach the point of perfect accomplishment before he hears plenty of "praise-in-anticipation."

We can learn that fear often parades as anger.

We can learn that all of us are naturally drawn to love and that that natural attraction can do more to mold behavior than the fear of punishment and pain will ever do.

We can learn to take time to figure out creative ways to help one another overcome problems through love.

We can learn how to make this a better, more harmonious world for dogs and people.

AFTERWORD

I have now shown you why dogs deserve dialogue and how they can indeed learn to hang on the words of their human partners. Dialogue is really so simple. People frequently ask me if I will give them "advanced lessons." They are usually a little startled when I answer that there is nothing more I can teach them, nothing more for them to learn. The language for clear human/dog dialogue, when practiced consistently over time, serves all the purposes for guiding dog behavior. I have written this book using nothing more than the 26 letters of the alphabet. Just as the alphabet is entirely adequate for written communication in the English language, the dialogue with your dog explained in this book meets all of the communication needs of any companion dog.

Now it is up to you to initiate this dialogue with your dog and practice it. Dialogue is not magical or mysterious, even though one dog owner did ask me if I used magic with her dog! Dialogue may appear to be magical in effect only because we have not understood what dogs really need. By applying what you have learned from this book, you have the means of effecting changes in many lives, dog and human. There will be many great success stories, and I want to hear about them. Please share with me how you were able to use what you learned from this book. Also please let me know how the book can be improved to make it more helpful.

Next I want to compile stories of shelter dogs which have been successfully adopted and integrated into permanent homes with the help of WR-DOS. Adopt a dog from an animal shelter, install WR-DOS, develop a priceless partnership, and send me your story.

APPENDIX A
Why "Pack Behavior" Is Irrelevant

There seems to be a nearly universal fascination among dog trainers with the wild canine pack behavior which seems to be reflected in the behavior of pet dogs. Many trainers have concluded that the relationship between a pet dog and his human partner is strongly influenced by the dog's instinctive "pack behavior." On the contrary, however, my experience has shown me that pack behavior is just about irrelevant to this relationship. Throughout this book I make clear the importance of replacing a dog's reliance on the demands of his instincts with reliance on a clear dialogue with his human partner.

Pack behavior is based on a dog's instinctive impulses toward establishing a social hierarchy (often with himself aspiring to a position of dominance). Such behavior only appears in the human-dog relationship when the dog has no other way to relate to a human than as if the human were a dog. In other words, if the dog exhibits what is called pack behavior, it is only because he has been given no other means of decision-making than his instincts and knows no other way of meeting his needs.

Probably the most important element of pack behavior is competition—competition for those things which fulfill a canine's basic needs. In the kind of human-dog relationship I have advocated in this book, pack behavior becomes irrelevant because the human takes on his rightful responsibility for meeting *all* the dog's needs. Most dog owners supply the dog's material need for food, toys, shelter, and so forth. With dialogue, humans can also meet the dog's *greatest* need—his need for complete answers to his questions regarding life in a human society. When he has these answers, he gains self-confidence, self-esteem, and security. Where all the dog's needs are met, the expression of competitive hierarchy fades away. Dominant-submissive behavior literally disappears among the dogs I work with because dialogue makes it obsolete.

You may be wondering whether pack behavior influences your dog's relationship with other dogs. A dog which lacks dialogue with a human partner associates with another dog in only a dog-to-dog relationship. In such a relationship, elements of pack behavior may govern the actions of both dogs. And the results may be unpleasant if they are both, by nature, dominant or "alpha" dogs. (Alpha denotes a pack leader.) However, when one dog is already engaged in dialogue with a human partner, his behavior is no longer influenced by an instinctive desire to dominate another dog. The overriding influence on his behavior in this as in all situations is no longer his instincts, but rather the information he receives from his human partner. Such a dog no longer has dog-to-dog relationships. He has dog-to-human-dog relationships. If all the dogs involved in an encounter have dialogue with a human partner, pack behavior completely disappears.

I see the evidence of this dissolving of dominance every day in my own yard. I dogsit dogs in a home-care manner which at busy times requires several dogs from different homes to share common spaces. Experience has proven to me that dogs with an impulse for dominant behavior will not readily share anything. By limiting my dogsitting to only those dogs which have had WR-DOS training, I have eliminated problems with dominant dog behavior. Occasionally I have a half dozen or more dogs of a variety of temperaments at my home. They never express problematic pack behavior but show affection and care to each other as they share beds, toys, and my attention peacefully.

APPENDIX **B**
Solutions to Five Specific Problems

The exercises detailed in this book give you the means for eliminating problem dog behavior of all kinds. There are, however, five specific instances of undesirable behavior for which I use very definitive procedures which supplement the exercises which are the components of dialogue.

Jumping Up

Dialogue is fundamental to overcoming this problem behavior as it is with any other. Often a dog jumps up on people because of his frantic insecurity. The **Stay** exercises provide therapy for such a dog to gain control of his actions while at the same time he is developing confidence and overcoming his anxiety and insecurity. Use the specific technique I outline here for eliminating jumping *only* in conjunction with the confidence-building procedures of dialogue.

Position yourself, facing your dog, with one leg bent slightly and somewhat behind the other.

Carry on an energetic, approving conversation with your dog as you stand this way.

Continually face the dog. Pivot as necessary on the unbent leg.

When the dog jumps up on you, you are going to do one thing only—suddenly go to the ground.

When you get to the ground, you are going to pick up your dog and comfort him. Why will he be on the ground? Because on your way to the ground, your bent leg came forward and connected with him, knocking him to the ground.

Position yourself in front of your dog again and resume the energetic, approving conversation.

Repeat #4 and #5 in exactly the same manner if your dog jumps up again.

This is another example of setting up a circumstance from which the dog can learn. In this circumstance, as with others we have used, you are *not* scolding the dog or doing anything punishing to him. Your approving conversation blends right into a most sympathetic exclaiming, "WHAT HAPPENED TO YOU, POOR PUPPY, POOR GOOD PUPPY?" and so forth. All the dog knows is that *something*, he does not know what, knocked him down, and you were immediately there comforting him. Therefore, in his mind you and he are still on the same team, united against the unknown.

Some dogs will try the jumping a couple of times just to see if the unknown goblin gets them again. However, I have used this procedure with many dogs which never jumped on me a second time. Each one sat in front of me as I once again talked to him energetically while standing at the ready. But as he sat there, visibly working to contain his impulse to jump up, he frequently glanced over his shoulder. Obviously, he felt no threat from me but rather was still trying to figure out where the undetected goblin had come from!

If you connect with your dog with your knee and pause there, upright, for even a second, you have changed the entire nature of the circumstance. If you blurt out a correction—a correcting tone or a "no" or anything similar, you also have changed the circumstance. Your dog will perceive, and rightly, that you are unhappy with him. He will suffer the negative consequences of punishment for no gain. There is a high probability he will not even pause in his jumping. He will just jump and duck.

One owner of a very insecure big dog had tried all the punishment techniques for curbing jumping, all to no avail. After we had commenced building this dog's confidence for a few days, I demonstrated what the owner could do for the jumping. This dog never jumped up again from that day on. The owner was incredulous. What they had been fighting for a year, I had eliminated in three minutes, *without punishment.*

Housebreaking

People use many different methods for housebreaking a puppy or dog. I do not claim to have all the answers, but based on my own experience and the feedback from others whom I have advised, it appears the following ideas work very well and very quickly.

Three basic premises hold particularly well for the young puppy:

1. Puppies sleep a lot.
2. As soon as they wake up, puppies want to relieve themselves.
3. Puppies do not want to relieve themselves in their sleeping space.

Based on these premises, this is the quick and effective method for housebreaking:

Confine the puppy to a space no larger than what he needs in order to comfortably lie down to sleep. Barricades or a cage or kennel can be used. Locate this space where you can observe the puppy.

Observe the puppy at all times. As soon as the puppy wakes, he will begin to nose around and fret, trying to find a way to get out of his sleeping space so that he can relieve himself.

Respond instantly and take the puppy outside, saying something like "Do you want to go out?" The puppy will start to pick up on words like this very quickly along with the experience of the observer solving his problem for him very nicely. Within a few times of waking, he will begin to wake and immediately look for the observer's appearance, perhaps even making noises to attract the observer's attention. He will have figured out that this is the way to solve his problem, not trying to find a way out of the sleeping space for himself.

After several more times of getting this *consistent* reaction to his waking and making noises, the puppy will probably be ready to be outside the sleeping space safely. He will wake and *seek out* someone to take him outside. That someone, upon seeing him wake (he should still be observed at this point), should immediately go to his rescue, saying those now familiar words about going out. With *absolute consistency* in setting up this response pattern, housebreaking can take as little as a couple of days. The consistency has to be there during the night as well. The puppy has to be confined for nighttime right next to the observer's bed so that his waking will hopefully wake the sleeping person. That person will accompany him outside. Young puppies cannot "hold it" all night.

With the older puppy or adult dog there is the significant advantage that he does not need to relieve himself as often. Again, keep him confined unless you are directly playing with him. When playing, monitor his activity so that he gets no chance to relieve himself indoors. This is the way the dog will develop a consistent pattern of relieving himself only when he is outside. As with young puppies, if your response is absolutely consistent, it only takes a couple of days for the dog to comprehend that you will take him outside whenever he feels he needs to relieve himself. Older dogs actually learn more quickly to ask for your response.

Light Line Conditioning

Use of a light line can be essential with dogs which are evasive, which simply means that they are hard to get a hand on in an emergency. Some dogs are evasive because they are insecure and fear even the hand of a friend. Others may seem to have what I have referred to as doggy attention deficit disorder. For whatever reason, if your dog consistently breaks away from you and can only be caught by being trapped, he requires a light line as a safety precaution until his response to you develops.

A light line is just that, a very light line. I have successfully used a 1/8" nylon cord about 30 feet long for a 100-pound dog. The cord is snapped or tied to the dog's regular buckle collar, never to a chain training collar. The dog drags this line around 24 hours a day. It is so light that he soon forgets it is there at all. For use in the house, a light line about 10 to 15 feet long is appropriate.

Whenever you want to walk up to your dog, be sure you have the light line in your hand. Do not pull your dog to you with this line. The line should be slack as you approach your dog. But if the dog wants to remain out of your reach, you can work your way to him along the light line which will now be taut because the dog is moving away from you. Always be giving praise-in-anticipation. The only point you are making to your dog is that he cannot get away from you, and it is futile to try. You should never give him any reason to fear your approach. After you have successfully walked up to him this way many times, the habit of remaining in place as you approach will have overridden his impulse to pull away.

If when on leash your dog responds to the **Come** command instantaneously and without fail, but, when he is off leash, he splits the scene when he hears **Come**, start practicing this exercise using a 20 to 30 foot long leash. This longer leash is *not* a light line. It is a regular leash weight and is attached to the chain training collar because you are using it in specific practice of an exercise. Practice over time until the dog flies to you instantaneously and without fail from as much as 30 feet away. Then resume attempts at doing the recall off leash, first from six feet away, and gradually increase the distance . If your dog does not consistently move straight to you when you give the command **Come**, even from a distance of six feet, he needs to wear a light line until he progresses.

Practice the recall with the dog off leash but wearing his light line. Before giving the command **Come**, plant your foot firmly on top of the light line. When you give the command, if your dog does not make a move toward you as you give exuberant praise-in-response, tug on the light line to get him moving. If he then keeps moving toward you, ignore the light line, leave it on the ground under your foot, and complete the exercise as you would any other off-leash recall. If the situation is worse, and your dog completely ignores you by taking off in another direction when he hears the command **Come**, pick up the light line that is under your foot and reel him in (praising all the while) to complete the exercise. Sooner or later your dog will realize that somehow he never can get away, if for some reason that is what he wants to do when he hears **Come**. Again, you are creating a circumstance from which he can learn.

When you can judge that your dog is beginning to feel that running away is futile, you can start shortening the light line. Periodically clip a few inches off the end. Whether your dog was being evasive to your approach or was slow to respond to the command **Come**, as he improves, you can shorten the line because you know you can get closer to him before having to rely on the line.   Eventually, when you no longer need to use the line at all as your handle on the dog, he may simply have six inches of nylon cord dangling from his collar. That decoration may be there forever. For some dogs that six inches is enough to remind them of the light line and the fact that somehow and in some way that line always guaranteed that they could not get away from people. I estimate that only about two percent of dogs I have worked with have required light line conditioning.

Assault Behavior

There is only one situation in which I react to a dog's behavior negatively. That is in the case of unprovoked vicious assault by the dog on a person or another dog. Even then, my goal is to interrupt the thought pattern, not to berate or punish the dog.

If a dog attacks another dog or person while we are practicing obedience exercises, I immediately lift the dog off his feet by his chain collar. I hold the dog in the air for about five seconds. It seems like an eternity, believe me! But it is necessary. One or two seconds would be ineffective. Five seconds is not long enough to do any physical damage to the dog, but it is long enough that the dog *thinks* he may never get to draw another breath. This definitely interrupts his thoughts about attacking. At the end of the five seconds, I resume whatever I had been doing with the dog. No scolding, just more positive, productive training activity.

This procedure has never failed in my experience to eliminate assault behavior. It is sometimes difficult to help an owner commit himself or herself to employing this procedure. Of course it is never pleasant to watch a dog feeling very frightened by being hung for five seconds. And it is very hard to love your dog and know what a good dog he is and still have to be the one to do the hanging. But when the dog has a problem so extreme that he viciously attacks, it is the only choice and is only used to supplement the confidence-building dialogue. Remember, the five-second hanging does no permanent harm to him. However, if he bites someone and that person prosecutes, the court will demand the dog's destruction. That hurts permanently!

Using Crates

Sometimes anxiety-driven dog behavior can be very destructive. Giving such a dog dialogue has proved to be the solution. But while dialogue eliminates many behavior problems very quickly, even dialogue cannot replace anxieties instantaneously. A dog, however, can destroy a lot of property in a very few hours. During the time you are building your dog's confidence and peace of mind through dialogue, you must take practical steps to protect your home and possessions.

Crating your dog is an immediate, non-punishing way to protect your home from your dog's destructive behavior. Dogs enjoy having their own personal space to which they can resort when only the comfort of their bed will do. If for a time your dog must be in a crate not by his choice, but by yours, be sure that his crate is a very enjoyable and comfortable space. Place the crate near to wherever you are so that the dog does not associate the crate with isolation. Wire crates do little to obstruct the dog's observation by sight, hearing and smell of all that is going on around him.

Never put your dog in his crate as a punishment. If he associates the crate with punishment, it will not be a space he enjoys. There are those people who feel crates are inhumane and should never be used for a dog. I agree with them *if* the crate represents unpleasantness and punishment to the dog. Confining a dog to a space which he only associates with unhappiness is not progressive, productive or loving for the dog. So be sure that your dog associates his crate with cozy comfort, approval from you, and even a special toy or treat.

Once your dog feels at home in his crate, you can begin using it whenever you have to be away from your dog. Dogs which, because of insecurity, suffer separation problems when you are gone actually feel more peaceful and secure within the confines of their crate, their private, protected space. As your dog gains confidence and feels more secure about life, confining him in his crate when you must leave him alone at home will undoubtedly become a thing of his past. But chances are, he will still enjoy using his crate by choice as a quiet place of refuge.

APPENDIX C
Student Comments

Dogs are each so different. Our dogs, Mac and Kai, have personalities and behaviors so different it reminds one of the saying "Men are from Mars and women are from Venus". Those differences, however, don't negate the wisdom in Judy Moore's training techniques. The principles work, whether applied to animal or human.

D. Russell
Honolulu, Hawaii

It's the best money I've ever spent, and Judy's technique is the most humane and relationship-building method. It's one thing to have an obedient dog, but totally wonderful to have an obedient, loving buddy! It's so much more than *just* obedience school. Judy gave Kia and me a basis to build a beautiful dog-human relationship! I saw that Kia can be the well-mannered, well-behaved dog I wish her to be as soon as *I* learn how to bring it out in her. The hard work and patience Judy gave us won't be in vain! She has given us the foundation to grow on! I recommend her highly to all and believe her method is the best method of training. It works on all dogs.

D. Webb
Buena Vista, Colorado

Jussi had learned a lot during that summer with Judy in Aspen. It was amazing that in such a short time Judy managed to make him follow and heel, and sit, and down and all those basic commands. It was great for Jussi and for us.

J. Crosa
Portland, Oregon

Although my Airdale Mattie and I have been in training only four months, I've noticed a significant positive difference in her behavior. She is much more focused.

R. Osberg
Salida, Colorado

Nyka's got it; we are the ones who need the training.

D. Rhodes
Salida, Colorado

The program has been a *big* asset to me and my dog. Toshe began Judy's program at 3-1/2 months. She is now six months old, and whether we are at home, on the road, or in public, I find Toshe very eager to please.

K. Hicks
Buena Vista, Colorado

Through the years I have taken several dog obedience courses. This is the method that works. Judy's method is very simple and basic, and the results are wonderful. My dog is a very active animal and has a mind of her own. But once she is put on command, she becomes calm and manageable. We live in the country, but when I take the dog into town, people always comment on how well behaved she is.

J. Kratky
Nathrop, Colorado

Judy Moore's training was a tremendous help when we adopted a large, grown dog from the shelter. It is a real delight to have a well-trained dog. Dog and owners are happier and can go on more adventures together.

N. Ayers
Buena Vista, Colorado

Kashtin seems a lot happier, and she obeys ten times better than ever before. If a cat takes off and she wants to give chase, you can call her and she'll come, no if's, and's or but's about it.

C. Cates
Buena Vista, Colorado

Teddy was so frightened when we adopted him from the shelter. WR-DOS training helped me to know how to establish the initial relationship with a dog to keep him safe. I can go three weeks without practicing, and he doesn't forget any of the exercises.

J. Typer
Buena Vista, Colorado

After his first training session, Denali was responding to Judy as if he had had some prior training. I know he has had no other training. It was amazing to watch.

J. Gilden
Buena Vista, Colorado

An Amusing Account

I say that WR-DOS is character-building for the owner, and indeed it is. Kachina, however, belongs to someone who is already quite a character. Her owner, in addition to being a character, is a published writer. He wrote a history of his trials and tribulations with Kachina. This account illustrates the fact that even when a dog owner has trouble dedicating himself to the necessary precision, progress can be made with a difficult dog. The story may be encouraging for some readers, and entertaining for all.

Kachina and I may be one of the toughest teams Judy Moore has ever had to teach, but I can see the difference each week. We're both becoming more obedient. I tend to be too laid back about where my dog is going and therefore react slowly—waiting and hoping she will return to her proper place on her own. Kachina knows this and takes all the liberty I allow, and a little more.

She knows when Tuesday arrives. I ask if she wants to go "to class," and she runs to her leash and collar, sits, and waits for me to "change her necklace." She ignores distractions in the house and front yard and goes with me—off leash—to the car where she politely waits for permission to enter.

She no longer pukes from fear but reclines leisurely on the back seat for the half-hour ride to Buena Vista. At each corner, she pops up to ensure I'm on course—as promised—to class. If I change the route, Kachina knows immediately. She stands, surveys passing landscape, and then fixes me with an accusing eye, doing everything she can to tell me my navigational compass is out of whack.

Some nights she just can't wait to get to class. She crawls into the front seat, leans far forward and pushes her nose hard against the windshield, as if that will get her there sooner. She loves dogs she has been in class with for long months, can't wait to see Judy, and keeps an eye out for "new kids on the block."

She tests each new arrival with a modified version of her badger grim (teeth only, no snarl). If she is met with indifference or equal intimidation, she writes off the newcomer as not worthy of her efforts. Occasionally she meets a puppy with whom she would like to play. Her overtures are rough, fast and unrefined. She often scares the potential playmate—but she doesn't seem to glory in the fact as she used to.

Kachina most enjoys "confusion time" in class. On a "down-stay" command, she eagerly anticipates people running past and over her and occasionally stopping to pet her. She knows that staying put will result in lots of attention from nice people.

Although Tippy may be "official" educational assistant and demonstrator, Kachina has set herself up (via the seniority system) as unofficial worrier. She watches carefully as each dog threads the line. Those working well, she ignores. She visibly shows disdain for those causing problems. If they play more than she thinks they should, Kachina becomes digusted and squirms noticeably. She seldom breaks command, but it's obvious she wants to herd the other dog through the line "correctly."

Although Kachina easily sees fault in others, she conveniently ignores it in herself. Working off leash, she does well when she is between the wall of the barn and me. If she is on the inside of the circle and can see Tippy (Judy's lovable canine assistant) in the center of the arena with Judy, Kachina wanders toward them, knowing Tippy will react. At times Kachina tries to make up for past intimidations, but Tippy still isn't convinced her overtures are honest.

We can trust Kachina with strangers if she is on a command. We don't release her until she has "met" the stranger, and danger is past. At home, she no longer needs a muzzle when she's around people—just a command. She still isn't trustworthy around our fast-moving grandchildren or our older son Shane, but we're working on that. For some reason, there are still a few people who send out bad vibes that trigger her nasty streak, but she controls it. She's becoming a "good dog."

But it wasn't always this way. Kachina was a canine in danger. I was ready to send her to some rancher for a life of hard labor—or worse, to a cannery. She is smart—too smart—and has a mind of her own. She has a truly mean streak born of temerity.

We met Kachina at her birth place on a ranch early in 1995. Hind legs spread wide behind her, a tiny black and white ball of fur squirmed and quivered on the floor, leaving a wet mark on the tile. "Her mother is shy and a little snappy," the owner explained, "but she's a hell of a cow dog. This one should be the same." I looked at my wife, Terry, and the kids, Jodi and John, and knew no matter what I said, we weren't going to leave without the nine-week-old Border Collie pup. For the first time in my life, I bought a dog. All the others were rescued from some calamity.

The pup got car sick. There was a heated discussion concerning a name. At home, she cowered on the carpet, legs stretched behind her—making a wet streak again. "How much fluid can this dog emit?" I wondered. Time passed. I was willing to call her "Dog" (or Ralph because she still upchucked in the car) just to end the name arguments. Meanwhile, we wondered if the animal could use her hind legs or if we'd bought a cripple.

She stood up more often. We realized she was scared—of us, of the cat, of everything. Because the family is steeped in southwestern Pueblo Indian lore, we gave up on conventional names and began running through tags like Hopi, Kiva and Pueblo. When someone suggested Kachina (Hopi spirits present in steam, clouds and moisture), it seemed to fit. This bell-dragging, piddling, ball of fur seemed to embody a little of the spirit of many past pups.

She gained use of her back legs after a confrontation with Cricket, our cat. Cricket let Kachina win just to gain a playmate. Time passed, Kachina grew, and she began puppy purloining socks and other clothing. She dragged them behind the couch in the living room—a dark, hard-to-reach spot she called her own.

She learned that curling her lips and showing lots of teeth—in a convincing imitation of a badger—allowed her to have her way.

When one of us had the audacity to persist in retrieving stolen goods, she struck like a rattlesnake. It was a nasty habit I'd never had to contend with in a dog before. The kids were young and wanted to get down to Kachina's level to play. They had to be a little quicker than the pup or teeth marks were the consequence.

Kachina's herding instinct was strong and humorous. She herded anything—butterflies, flies, water from the hose, her people, and birds that took wing long before she could push them into a corner. Her ball was bigger than she was, and she herded it with her nose and front paws. (She's now graduated to a soccer ball).

Kachina, we realized, was a coward. Like people, she covered the fact by being "snappy." One day John left his mini-trampoline in the back yard. Kachina roared out the back door, skidded to a stop, and began her most vicious badger attack at the immobile trampoline—but wouldn't approach closer than ten feet. It took several days, much coaxing and many careful introductions before she accepted the intruder. On another occasion, Terry left a sack of potatoes in the hall near Kachina's dish. The dog went into a snarling, snapping fit—something new again invaded her territory.

The mean streak got worse, no matter how much affection or attention was lavished on Kachina. She attacked a neighbor child with no provocation. She dove at our own kids. Guests were not welcome in her house, and she lunged at visitors (usually strangers) who reached toward her in greeting. Terry frequently braved flashing teeth to retrieve something Kachina appropriated. The dog snarled and snapped at me—an attitude I never saw in previous dogs I've owned.

This behavior wasn't tolerable, and we were thinking of giving Kachina to a large ranch where flashing hooves of some mossy horned bovine might knock some sense into her. Besides, people on ranches wear boots and Levis, armoring the range of her sharp teeth. All my past dogs seemed to train themselves. They learned to sit, to stay down, and greet strangers with noise rather than with the attitude and enthusiasm of an attack dog.

Terry spotted an advertisement in the classified section of the newspaper. It said something about saving dogs through training and promised results. She suggested Kachina and I could each stand to learn some obedience. Within a week we were in Judy Moore's barn watching a one-year-old dog lose her attitude. First, Judy didn't react to intimidation. When the private lesson began, Judy simply disappeared every time Kachina showed signs of wanting to exercise her control over the stranger at the other end of the leash. At the end of a half-hour, they were fast friends. When Judy reached for her, there were no teeth, just a happy tail wag— "Hey, this attention stuff is pretty good!" It really looked easy.

A couple of days later, it was my turn. I twisted and turned, Judy pleaded and explained, and I stumbled, wobbled, and thought I was learning to disappear quickly and completely. But we hadn't yet been to group therapy. As dogs entered the barn that first night, Kachina took it upon herself to attack each one, regardless of size. Her bluff worked in every case. Timid little Tippy was so intimidated within a few minutes that, two years later, she is still apprehensive around Kachina.

Lacking a fenced yard in which to practice at home, Kachina and I used the county road. I spun and twisted and disappeared until I was so dizzy I couldn't walk. When a car passed, herding instinct took over and Kachina did her radial ripping best to catch it. September 27, 1996, we were at the foot of our driveway. I was spinning and (I thought) disappearing, and Kachina was doing pretty much as she pleased. (Disappearing, you see, is supposed to worry the dog and make it attentive to me.) Terry (Mom) drove by with a word of greeting and a wave. Kachina made a quick loop around me and hit the end of her leash, tying my legs like a calf at a branding fire. I went down hard on the pavement, slowing my fall with my right arm. As I muttered to the blacktop, a vehicle approached and stopped. I looked up and saw the Salida Police Department shield on the side of the pickup and the words "Animal Control." The officer was a neighbor on his way home.

A voice from above asked, "Are you OK?"

"Yeah. I'll get up when I get my breath back," I grunted. I wasn't really ready, but I proved my point just to get rid of the embarrassing observer. I began spinning and disappearing like a dervish. Dizzy, shaken, embarrassed, angry, I didn't notice the pain. Kachina and I finished our lesson and 20 minutes later went into the house. The arm stiffened through dinner, and I finally consented (Terry said I was learning obedience) to a trip to the hospital. Sure enough, the arm was broken.

I returned to class the following Tuesday, wearing a cast. After her first success, Kachina dumped me several more times. Aided by soft tanbark in the arena, I learned to fall without landing on my arm. More embarrassment. Slow learner that I am, I realized I was doing something wrong. Judy coached, and I learned the secret of truly disappearing. Judy suggested a muzzle (nose ribbon) for Kachina so if she got loose in class she couldn't eat Tippy or another paying customer. I agreed. I was learning obedience. I was still thinking of a kennel at the cannery, but not as often.

After two years in class, Kachina is a different dog. She's not ready to give up her headstrong ways enough to work reliably off leash, but on leash she has manners and enjoys meeting people. Small dogs who show temerity are still at risk of receiving the badger grim and a growl of intimidation from within her nose ribbon, but she doesn't attack. Dogs and people who stand their ground become quick friends.

Dogs come and go from class—most learning patience and self-control much faster than Kachina. We've become the slowest learners—the old hands—but we continue because each week brings new challenges, new dogs, new people, and Kachina loves it, in spite of herself. Judy and I look back at the charging, snarling, vicious animal that entered her barn and realize there's been a world of improvement. As Kachina gains confidence that the world isn't out to get her, she becomes a more playful, loving, trustworthy dog.

Wolf Hybrids as Companion Dogs

Even while a very vocal contingent in this country attempts to obstruct the reintroduction of wolves into some areas where they originally roamed free, other people are domestically breeding wolf/dog hybrid puppies to supply a ready market for pet wolf-dogs. We need to protect wolves in the wild and guarantee them the habitat that is rightfully theirs. But these magnificent creatures should not be domestically bred to satisfy man's desire for exotic pets.

There is a great gamble involved in breeding wolf/dog hybrids. A wolf/dog hybrid puppy is going to be born with a combination of traits from the wolf and the dog. If he happens to get the sociability of the wolf and the human orientation of the dog, he will be a fantastic animal. But if his makeup is dominated by the non-human orientation of the wolf, he will not fit in to the domestic human scene successfully at all. When he outgrows cute puppyhood and is a large, strong adult, he may exhibit aggressive tendencies for which he will be destroyed.

Even a "successful" hybrid with the human orientation of a dog may have too many other wolf traits to successfully fit in as a pet in a human household. Hybrids which are over three-quarters wolf find the physical constraints of urbanized human society very difficult to adjust to. Few people can provide the immense open spaces which these near-wolf hybrids need for their mental and physical well-being. There are at least three sanctuaries in Colorado alone which provide refuge for the products of this wolf hybrid domestic breeding.

People get a hybrid pup because, like all babies, a pup is appealing. But in several months these people realize the pup is becoming a very large animal which they are not prepared to handle and care for. It is hard enough for people to dedicate themselves to solving behavior problems in their dogs in order to prevent abandonment. And dogs are initially humanly oriented and want to please people. It can take infinitely more effort and dedication to meet the training needs of a wolf hybrid that has little human orientation! So the young wolf hybrids are abandoned at an even greater rate than are dogs.

There is yet another issue to be considered in keeping a near-wolf hybrid as a pet. Perhaps there *are* a few individuals who can provide adequate space to maintain a near-wolf hybrid comfortably. But it is doubtful whether these people have this space sufficiently isolated from civilization. Understand, while some humans are fascinated with the thought of wolves as pets, others are still brainwashed to believe that wolves are somehow evil and undesirable.

We live in a world where even wild wolves are being denied the right to habitat and life in all but a few areas of North America. It is almost impossible to adequately protect a domestic near-wolf hybrid from deadly encounters with human society. If an animal looks like a wolf, he has a bounty on his head in the minds of many people. A near-wolf hybrid must always obey humans' rules for dogs, but often his normal wolf behavior is impossible to curtail short of total imprisonment. It is a lose-lose situation. He was bred to be wolf-like, he looks like a wolf, but he must live by the rules for domestic dogs. If a near-wolf hybrid's behavior infringes on one of the laws governing dogs, he gets no second chance.

I know. I tried to provide a home and sanctuary for a domestically bred near-wolf hybrid which had to be given up at adulthood by his original owner. He had all the best traits of both wolf and dog and was a most loving, benign companion animal. He deserved to live. But to guarantee him life, I would have had to keep him securely penned at all times because even though my home includes space for a wolf to run, it is not isolated from the eyes of other people. Our land is shared by wildlife of many kinds. Among other things, dogs are forbidden to run among and mingle with some of this wildlife. Domestic wolf hybrids are governed by dog laws. Our hybrid had no way to know that. The domestic wolf hybrid we had tried so hard to provide with a good life, against the odds, was cut down without warning in the prime of his life by humans—the same creatures who had thoughtlessly brought him into being, bringing him into a world that had no place for him.

APPENDIX F
Rescue Organizations

The American Humane Association
63 Inverness Drive East
Englewood CO 80112 (303) 792-9900

American Humane Education Society
350 S. Huntington Avenue
Boston MA 02130 (617) 522-7400

American Society for the Prevention of Cruelty to Animals
441 E. 92nd Street
New York NY 10128 (212) 876-7700

Best Friends Animal Sanctuary
P.O. Box G
Kanab UT 84741 (801) 644-2001

Dedication and Everlasting Love to Animals (DELTA)
P.O. Box 9
Glendale CA 91209

The Doris Day Animal League
900 2nd Street NE, Suite 303
Washington DC 20002 (202) 842-3325

Friends of Animals, Inc.
P.O. Box 1244
Norwalk CT 06856 (203) 866-5223

The Humane Society of the United States

2100 L Street NW
Washington DC 20037 (202) 452-1100

The MaxFund Animal Adoption Center
1025 Galapago Street
Denver CO 80204-3942 (303) 595-4917

National Humane Education Society
521A East Market Street
Leesburg VA 22075 (703) 777-8319

North Shore Animal League
Lewyt Street
Port Washington NY 11050

Pet Adoption Fund
7515 Deering Avenue
Canoga Park CA 91303-1407

Pets Are Wonderful Council (P.A.W.)
500 N. Michigan Avenue, Suite 200
Chicago IL 60611 (312) 836-7145

APPENDIX G
Recommended Reading

Dog Adoption by Joan Hustace Walker
    ICS Books, Inc.: 1996 Excellent guide urging adoption of
    adult dogs and giving all the tips as to where, why and how.

The Adoption Option by Eliza Rubenstein and Shari Kalina
    Howell Book House: 1996 Instructions and advice for how to
    find and adopt a dog.

Real Lives: eleven teenagers who don't go to school by Grace
    Llewellyn, ed.
    Lowry House: 1993 Acclaimed as "a book to set people free."

Dialogue by Linda Ellinor and Glenna Gerard
    John Wiley and Sons, Inc.: 1998 Captivating treatise on the
    transforming power of conversation from which dogs, as well
    as humans, can benefit.

abandoned: 71, 105

abuse: 43, 45, 67, 151

adoption: 145-146

aggression: 27, 55, 59, 151

aggressive: 149, 151, 175

AKC Novice Level exercises: 46

alien: 34
    culture: 34
    world: 35

alpha: 157

animal shelter: 48, 74, 105, 149, 155

animal shelters: 43, 57

answers: 11

attention: 22, 27, 43, 50-52, 62, 74, 76, 161, 170

attentiveness: 36, 50, 52, 63-64, 76-77, 90, 129

attitude: 21, 59, 61, 66, 77, 103, 117, 172-173

bad dog: 13

behavior: 22, 92, 94, 105, 125, 145
    impulsive: 30, 63, 64
    problem: 40, 44, 75, 92

problems: 145-148, 164, 176

behavior consulting: 4

behavior problems: 145-146, 151, 164, 176

blind dogs: 53

body language: 100, 107

body movement: 38, 70

body reflex: 38, 53-55, 133, 136

collar: 83, 161

Come: 37, 52, 133-142

commitment: 145, 147

communication: 76, 84, 94, 137, 139, 150, 155

confidence: 57, 59, 66, 68, 72-73, 75, 92, 105, 146, 158, 174

confident: 105

confusion: 13, 23, 27, 29, 55, 69, 73, 115, 129, 170

consistency: 69, 72, 97

consistent: 161

conversation: 49, 57, 65-66, 73, 75, 86, 104, 158, 180

correcting tone: 42, 48, 67, 68, 69, 72, 75, 87, 89, 98, 104, 109, 119, 132, 140, 159

crates: 164

deaf dogs: 53

dialogue: 4-5, 11-12, 79, 83, 85, 87, 89, 90, 94, 105, 131, 155, 164

dog operating system: 46-47

domination: 21, 28, 34, 41, 43, 48, 149

Down: 37, 55, 113-124

Down-stay: 37, 61, 113-124

downers: 113

Emotional IQ: 61-64

Emotional stability: 55, 105

energy level: 38, 106

fear: 5, 13

food treats: 40, 43

forging: 101

formal command: 72, 76, 85

frustrating: 23, 45

frustration: 13, 48, 55, 57

fundamental concepts: 31

gimmicks: 42

Heel: 37, 45, 75, 96-104

off leash: 37
on leash: 37
Sit-Stay: 37
homeless dogs: 147
Housebreaking: 160
human world: 12, 13
impulse: 22, 28-29, 30, 31, 56, 63,
  94, 105, 131, 157, 159, 162
individuality: 151
Indulgence: 31
informal command: 86
initiation of dialogue: 36-37, 41, 52,
  87, 89-90
instinct: 22, 29, 32, 36, 63
instinctive language: 22-23, 28, 62,
  64
instincts: 21, 156, 157
intelligence: 61-63, 151
job retraining: 27
jumping up: 158
language: 9, 11, 12, 76, 84, 155
leash: 51, 71, 78, 83, 85-86, 162, 174
Light Line: 161-163
mistakes: 32, 34, 71, 128, 153
negative reinforcement: 40, 42
obedience: 21, 49, 52, 62, 83, 163,
  166, 173-174
obedience exercises: 31, 44, 48, 55,
  73, 76, 163
one-eighty: 87, 89
pack behavior: 28, 29, 156
partnership: 31, 36, 155
peace of mind: 57, 164
permanent relationship: 148
permission: 30, 78, 169
personality: 22, 49, 72, 150
  temperamental: 150
  unique: 150
positive reinforcement: 40, 43
practice: 28, 29, 46, 55, 70, 72-74,
  78, 83-84, 91-92, 101, 105, 116,

125, 136, 155
praise-in-anticipation: 66-68, 71-72,
  153, 162
praise-in-response: 69, 162
preconceptions: 12
problem dog: 15
punishing: 23, 32, 41
punishment: 42, 71, 153, 159, 164
questions: 11
redeem: 11
reflex response: 70, 97
rehabilitation: 3
relationship: 74, 90, 156, 166
respect: 28, 31, 34, 39, 64, 151
rule book: 22, 30, 32, 35, 41, 55, 62
safety: 30, 37, 51, 86
scolding: 32, 40, 67, 71, 88, 103,
  159, 163
self-confidence: 23, 25, 32, 34, 61,
  108, 150, 156
self-esteem: 25, 32, 34, 55, 59, 64,
  72, 78, 88, 97, 148, 156
sensitivity: 63, 151
shelter dogs: 105, 146, 155
Sit: 37, 105-112
sniffing: 43, 72, 101
Stand: 37, 125-132
Stand-stay: 37, 125-132
standers: 116-117
submission: 21, 24
therapy: 49, 75, 173
traditional training: 11
training methods: 28-29, 39-41, 43
understanding: 94, 97, 149, 152
voice tone: 38, 65-66, 91, 102, 107,
  126
Wapiti Run: 3-4
wolf hybrids: 175-176
WR-DOS: 46-49, 54, 64, 69-70, 73-
  74, 76, 83, 98, 146-147, 150, 155,
  169

ORDER FORM

There are four convenient ways to order *Dogs Deserve Dialogue: Rover Should Hang on Your Words, NOT on your leash*, by Judy Moore:

Telephone orders: Local - (719) 395-8543 Toll Free - 1-888-262-0704
Have your credit card ready.

E-mail orders: dialogue@amigo.net

Fax orders: Include the information on the coupon below
and fax to 1-719-395-8543.

Postal orders: Use the following coupon for postal orders:

Please send _____ copies of *Dogs Deserve Dialogue: Rover Should Hang on Your Words, NOT on Your Leash*, by Judy Moore @15.95 each to:

I understand that I may return the book for a full refund for any reason, no questions asked.

Name:_____

Address:_____

City_____State:_____Zip:_____-_____

Sales Tax: Please add 3% for books shipped to Colorado addresses or 5% for books shipped to Chaffee County, Colorado addresses.

Shipping and Handling: $4.00 for the first book and $1.00 for each additional book. Free shipping and handling on orders of 10 books or more.

Priority mail: $5.00 for the first book and $2.50 for each additional book.

Total Amount Enclosed:_____

Circle payment type:
     Check
     Credit Card: Visa   MasterCard
     Card Number:_____
     Name on card:_____Exp.Date:_____/_____
     Signature:_____

Mail form to: **Tyke Publishing**
          P.O. Box 4132
          Buena Vista. CO 81211-4132 USA

Call toll-free and order now
Also visit **www.helpyourdog.com**